LAST LINE OF DEFENCE
New Zealanders Remember the War at Home

Also in this series:

Last Line of Defence

New Zealanders Remember the War at Home

Edited by Megan Hutching

Foreword by the Right Honourable Helen Clark

HarperCollins*Publishers*
in association with
the Ministry for Culture and Heritage

National Library of New Zealand Cataloguing-in-Publication Data
Hutching, Megan.
Last line of defence : New Zealanders remember the war at
home / edited by Megan Hutching ; foreword by Helen Clark.
ISBN-13: 978-1-86950-605-6
ISBN-10: 1-86950-605-7
1. World War, 1939-1945—Personal narratives, New Zealand.
2. World War, 1939-1945—New Zealand. 3. New Zealand—
History—1918-1945. I. Title.
940.548193—dc 22

First published 2007
HarperCollins*Publishers (New Zealand) Limited*
P.O. Box 1, Auckland

ISBN-10: 1 86950 605 7
ISBN-13: 978 1 86950 605 6

Set in Bembo

Cover design by Matt Stanton, HarperCollins Design Studio
Book design by Dexter Fry
Typeset by Janine Brougham
Printed by Everbest Printing, China

Main front cover photo: *WAAFs on coast-watching duty in North Auckland.* ATL, Evatt Collection, F-106389-1/2
Inset front cover photo: *Soldiers marching in camp.* ATL, New Zealand Free Lance Collection, PAColl-8602-41

This book is dedicated to my mother, Iris Hutching, who was a young wife with three small children during the war years. She has always told me about her life, and in doing so has shown what richness personal stories add to the history that people make.

FOREWORD

I am very pleased to welcome this book of personal accounts from people who served in New Zealand during the Second World War.

Last Line of Defence is the final in a series of books based on oral histories with veterans from the 1939–45 conflict. Fittingly, its focus is on those women and men who were charged with the task of protecting our country — they were New Zealand's last line of defence.

At the peak, over 70,000 New Zealanders were serving overseas during the war, but nearly 115,000 were in uniform at home. They were members of the Women's War Service Auxiliary, the Emergency Precautions Service, the Emergency Fire Service, or the home-based Army, Navy and Air Force; another 120,000 were in the Home Guard.

Defending New Zealand at home was a full-time role for some: driving trucks for the Army, patrolling the coast in Navy ships and Air Force planes, operating radios, working in supply. For others, war service came on top of their regular job; a hard day's work on the farm or in the factory followed by evenings on patrol for members of the Home Guard.

Oral histories help us begin to understand the anxieties and challenges, hopes and dreams of those who served on New Zealand soil for the duration of the war. They give us an insight into the breadth of the backroom tasks, so vital to the war overseas and the security of this country.

These are stories located far from the chaos of battle and the demands of frontline service, but they are no less a part of New Zealand's war history. Service and sacrifice in war takes many forms, including the refusal to take part in conflict.

I thank the people who have shared their stories with us in this book. I congratulate Megan Hutching and the team in the Ministry for Culture and Heritage for producing this book, and others in the series. *Last Line of Defence* is the story of New Zealand in the Second World War; I urge New Zealanders to read it to better understand the role of that event in our history.

Helen Clark
Prime Minister

CONTENTS

PREFACE

PREFACE

In *Footsteps: Adventures of a Romantic Biographer*, Richard Holmes wrote that the past is not simply 'out there' but lives 'most vividly in all of us, deep inside, and needs constantly to be given expression and interpretation'.

He went on to say that 'the lives of great artists and poets and writers are not, after all, so extraordinary by comparison with everyone else. Once known in any detail and any scope, every life is something extraordinary, full of particular drama and tensions and surprise, often containing unimagined degrees of suffering or heroism, and invariably touching extreme moments of triumph and despair, though frequently unexpressed. The difference lies in the extent to which one is eventually recorded, and the other is eventually forgotten' (p. 208). Although Holmes was writing about being a biographer, to me his words encapsulate how and why oral history is such a powerful means of restoring the 'ordinary' individual's experience to history.

This book is different from the six other volumes in this series in two ways: women's stories outnumber men's, and none of the people interviewed experienced frontline service. As a result, it is different in tone — the war work of people in this book was quiet, although not unremarkable, and so they do not recount life-threatening situations where they are under attack by troops or planes or ships of the enemy. However, theirs was important work that contributed to the fighting of the war. The exception is Merv Browne's story. Merv was a pacifist and became a conscientious objector, bravely refusing to participate in any aspect of fighting.

In order to find people to interview, I began by publicising the project and asking people who had served in uniform at home to get in touch. I sent those who responded a lengthy questionnaire, asking them about their experiences. I am extremely grateful to those who filled in my questionnaire either for themselves or on behalf of someone else. I have also been fortunate to receive accounts from people of their or their relative's experiences during the war, which I have very much appreciated.

Previous page: *Harbour defence motor launch* Q1183. Royal New Zealand Navy Museum, ABF0131

All of the questionnaires and other accounts that I have received will eventually be deposited with the Alexander Turnbull Library in Wellington, where they will be available to researchers. The recordings of the interviews and accompanying material will be archived at the Oral History Centre at the Alexander Turnbull Library. These, too, will be available to researchers, subject to any conditions placed on them by the interviewees.

The words that appear in this book are only some of those recorded in the interviews. I have tried to preserve the informal language of the interviews, because I want the stories to reflect the way people spoke, but each has been heavily edited for readability and content.

As usual, my colleagues at the Ministry's History Group have given me the benefit of their advice and knowledge. I am very grateful to them all, especially Ian McGibbon, who has shared his vast knowledge of the Second World War, David Green, and Bronwyn Dalley, for her usual helpful suggestions. Thanks too to Claire Taggart, who organised my travel when I was away interviewing, and whose interest in the books and their subjects reminds me again of why we have produced them.

I thank the Prime Minister, Helen Clark, for her ongoing interest in this series of books, which are a result of her initiative.

I also wish to thank Helen Phibbs in my home town of Warkworth, who gave me such useful background information on the WRNS; Joan McCracken, Heather Mathie and their colleagues at Turnbull Library Pictures; Paul Restall at the Navy Museum; Matthew O'Sullivan at the Air Force Museum; Elspeth Orwin at Auckland City Libraries; Linda Evans and the staff at the Alexander Turnbull Library's Oral History Centre; Ray Grover; Malcolm McKinnon; Lynn Benson; Marjorie Lee of the Ex-Wrens Association; and the team at HarperCollins, for their support and expertise, especially Sue Page, who edited the text.

As this is the last in a series of books, I want to reflect briefly on the experience of interviewing men and women about their wartime service. The war ended over 60 years ago, so they were remembering things which had happened a long time previously. Some incidents were as fresh in their minds as the day they had happened; at other times they were surprised at the seeming mundaneness of the things I wanted to know and had to search their memories.

They have shown me great hospitality — feeding me home baking (and gin!), giving me fruit, taking me out for meals. I have made some true friends. They have also displayed great trust — not only when I carried off their precious photographs for copying, but especially in the way they told me about their personal lives, knowing that significant parts of their stories would be published. At all times they were eager to take part in this project. In return, I hope that in the books — their books — I have managed to show, as Richard Holmes has remarked, that 'every life is something extraordinary'.

Megan Hutching
October 2006

GLOSSARY

AC1	aircraftsman, first class (rank in Air Force)
Anson	Avro Anson, a British twin-engine light transport and training aircraft
asdic	also known as 'sonar'; device for locating submarines by using sound waves; named after Anti-Submarine Detection Investigation Committee
ATC	Air Training Corps
Aunt Daisy	Maud Basham, who had a popular nationwide morning radio show
batwoman	female officer's female orderly
Bren	British light machine gun
button stick	wooden stick with slot in middle used to protect fabric when polishing brass uniform buttons
CB	confined to barracks
CO	conscientious objector *or* commanding officer
conchies	slang term for conscientious objectors
Corsair	Chance-Vought Corsair, a US single-engine fighter aircraft
coxswain	person who steers a ship and has charge of its crew
cutter	ship's boat used for transporting stores or passengers
Dakota or DC3	Douglas DC3 Dakota, a twin-engine aircraft, mostly used for transporting personnel and cargo
drogue	funnel- or cone-shaped device towed behind an aircraft as a target
erk	Air Force slang for ordinary serviceman or woman
galley	place where food is cooked or prepared
gantry	mezzanine
glengarry	hat with lengthwise crease
HD(ML)	Harbour defence (motor launch)
Jap(s)	Japanese
Jayforce	New Zealand force that took part in occupation of Japan after the Second World War

keeler	single-hull yacht with keel
kite	Air Force slang term for an aircraft
Kittyhawk	Curtiss-Wright Kittyhawk, a US single-engine fighter or fighter-bomber aircraft
Lancaster	Avro Lancaster, a British four-engine heavy bomber
Lewis gun	light machine gun
matelot	Navy slang for sailor
mess	place where food is eaten
MO	medical officer
NCO	non-commissioned officer
nylons	women's stockings
OC	officer commanding
OCTU	Officer Cadet Training Unit
OE	overseas experience
Oxford	Airspeed Oxford, a British multi-engine training aircraft
palliasse	mattress stuffed with straw
POW(s)	prisoner(s) of war
PTTS	Preliminary Technical Training School, Air Force
quartermaster	officer responsible for food, clothing and equipment of troops
RAP	Regimental Aid Post (first aid station)
reveille	bugle signal to get out of bed
RSA	Returned Soldiers'/Services Association
screw	slang for guard at conscientious objectors' detention camp
(Seddon) Tech	Seddon Memorial Technical College, Wellesley Street, Auckland
serge	finely woven woollen cloth
sked	schedule
skipper	person in command of a ship
SU	Servicing Unit
TB	tuberculosis
Third Div(ision)	3 New Zealand Division, which served in the Pacific
Tiger Moth	De Havilland Tiger Moth, a British biplane used for training pilots

TOC-I	target intercept(or)
Tommies	British servicemen
trench mortar	short-barrel cannon that fires shells at a high elevation over a short range
VAD(s)	(member(s) of) Voluntary Aid Detachment
VD	venereal disease
VE Day	Victory in Europe Day, 8 May 1945
Vickers	British heavy machine gun
VJ Day	Victory over Japan Day, 15 August 1945
VRD	Vehicle Reception Depot
WAAC(s)	(member(s) of) Women's Auxiliary Army Corps
WAAF(s)	(member(s) of) Women's Auxiliary Air Force
Waafery	accommodation for WAAFs
Wren(s)	(member(s) of) Women's Royal (New Zealand) Naval Service
Wrennery	accommodation for Wrens
WR(NZ)NS	Women's Royal (New Zealand) Naval Service
WWSA	Women's War Service Auxiliary
YMCA	(hall with recreational facilities run by) Young Men's Christian Association
YWCA	(hall with recreational facilities run by) Young Women's Christian Association

INTRODUCTION

IN UNIFORM
AT HOME

MERV BROWNE heard that Germany had invaded Poland when he was at the pictures in Wanganui one night in early September 1939. The news of the invasion was flashed onto the screen during the film. When he came out after the show, he said, 'I looked up to the sky, quite expecting there to be bombers coming over. I thought it was going to be like that. Of course it wasn't.'

The stories most often told about those in the armed forces during the Second World War are of battles fought, won and lost in overseas places that resonate in New Zealand's military history — Crete, El Alamein, Mono Island, Cassino — or in theatres such as the Mediterranean and North Atlantic convoys, the Battle of Britain, or the bombing raids over Germany. Sometimes the stories are of men who were taken prisoner of war.

However, a significant number of men and women who served in uniform did not go overseas. While some attention had been given to local defences as part of New Zealand's military preparations, especially during 1941, the main focus had been on training men for service in the Middle East or Europe. Defence of the homeland became an issue after the Japanese attack on the US naval base at Pearl Harbor in December 1941, because, especially after the subsequent Japanese capture of Singapore, the threat of invasion seemed very real.

One consequence was an increase in the number of men called up for service in New Zealand; another was the recruitment of women for the armed forces to free up men to serve overseas. Women enlisted as WAAFs, WAACs and Wrens, and by the time the war ended in August 1945 around 10,000 women had served. The number of people who served as New Zealand's last line of defence was large. By October 1942, there were over 107,000 people serving full-time in the home defence forces. The majority — around 82,000 — were in the Army, with 20,000 in the Air Force and nearly 5000 in the Navy. In addition, more than a quarter of a million people were involved in the Home Guard, Emergency

Previous page: *Members of the Emergency Precautions Scheme practise putting out a fire.* ATL, Evening Post Collection, PAColl-8557-44

Precautions Services (civil defence work), Emergency Fire Service and Women's War Service Auxiliary.

Men like Peter Crispe and Harry Spencer, whose stories appear in this book, served at home because they were deemed not fit for active service. While they may have preferred to go overseas, the work they did was essential to the running of the military machine. Others, like George Judge, served first in the armed forces at home and then overseas.

Most of the chapters in this book are based on interviews with women who served as WAACs, WAAFs and Wrens in the Army, Air Force and Navy, respectively. They worked in jobs similar to those they had held in civilian life — although some, such as Gwen Stevens and Betty van Praag, did work which, because of its secrecy, they could not discuss with their family and friends. Ngaire Gibbons seized the opportunities offered by the war to become a driver in the Army, moving trucks around the lower North Island. Hazel Rowe worked at one of the heavy anti-aircraft batteries around the coast. Maisie Takle was able to spend time nursing as a VAD in the Air Force, a career she had been denied in civilian life because she could not afford the training. Derek Laver also took advantage of wartime service to do something he had long wanted, and enlisted in the Navy, serving on a harbour defence motor launch in Wellington and Auckland as an asdic (sonar) operator, keeping an ear out for submarines. Kath Dyall and Heather Crispe worked in officers' messes in the Army and the Navy

Above: *WAACs operating a rangefinder, 1943.* ATL, New Zealand Free Lance Collection, F-71988-1/2

Left: *WAAFs covering a wing with fabric at Hobsonville air station, 1942.* RNZAF Official, via Air Force Museum, Christchurch, PR45

in Auckland, and Jane McIntyre had the gloriously titled job of batwoman to the senior WAAC officer at Papakura camp. George Clark, who was in a reserved occupation as a farmer, served his country by joining the local Home Guard unit, and combined serious training with rural adventures such as pig hunting. Maisie Munro worked as a telegraphist in the Navy, and became a petty officer after sitting exams whilst stationed at station ZLO in Waiouru.

All of the former servicemen and women in this book enlisted because they believed it was their duty to do so. It was a time when New Zealand's connections to Britain and its place in the British empire were taught in schools, when Britain was referred to as 'Home', and when the overwhelming majority of the Pakeha population was of British origin. It is hardly surprising that these young men and women felt they must take part in this war to help Britain — for King and country, as Jane McIntyre put it. That Merv Browne had the courage to refuse to take part is even more remarkable in a situation where patriotism was seen as being willing to go 'where Britain goes', as Prime Minister Michael Savage so memorably stated after Britain (and New Zealand) had declared war on Germany. It was a time when the war was the focus of everyone's lives, a war which was not unexpected, but which was anticipated with dread, especially by those with family members who had taken part in the First World War, the 'war to end wars', which had finished only 20 years before.

WAR IS DECLARED

THE COUNTRY WAS NOT WELL-PREPARED for war in September 1939. In May that year the Army's volunteer Territorial Force had comprised only 10,364 men. The National Military Reserve was established at this time, with all able-bodied men between the ages of 20 and 55 years required to register. The Territorial Air Force had 76 officers and 265 men, and the Navy had 7 officers and 688 other ranks on active service, with another 700 on loan from the Royal Navy. The combined numbers of the two naval reserve forces were similar.

Once war was declared, things quickly got moving. Three months' initial continuous training was introduced for Territorial units. Coastal artillery and anti-aircraft defences were manned at Auckland, Wellington and Lyttelton. Coast-watching stations were set up and manned with Navy, Army and Marine Department personnel. Army personnel provided guards on designated 'vital points', which included armed forces establishments, bulk oil installations and important wireless stations.

Three Army mobilisation camps to train men before they went overseas were established or extended, one in each of the country's three military districts. These were at Trentham near Wellington, Papakura near Auckland, and Burnham near Christchurch. Facilities at the camps included picture theatres,

Aerial view of Burnham camp. ATL, War History Collection, DA-12868

libraries, hospitals, dental hospitals, and wet and dry canteens run by the Canteen Board. By 1941, 23,483 men had received preliminary training and been sent overseas from these camps. In January of that year, infantry went for the first time into Waiouru camp, where they occupied a mixture of huts and bell tents. George Judge, who trained there in the winter of 1941, did not have a comfortable time under canvas: 'There wasn't much room in them. When you got frost, the canvas froze solid at night.'

The Navy also acted to protect New Zealand's ports. Three Auckland fishing trawlers were refitted as minesweepers to search the approaches for mines. A 24-hour Examination Service, run by the Royal Naval Volunteer Reserve and local harbour-board pilots, ensured that no enemy ships entered harbours undetected. The ships they used were manned by merchant seamen. The Naval Control Service ensured that merchant ships kept working, and organised them into convoys.

Most of the naval operations were based at Devonport on Auckland's North Shore. In January 1941, a naval training establishment was commissioned on Motuihe Island in the Hauraki Gulf. HMS *Tamaki* turned out 250 trained ratings three times a year, including seamen, signalmen, telegraphists, stokers and accountants. Derek Laver recalls that it was a good place to be in the summer, but that the discipline was very strict. 'Lovely beach, and in the summer it was great. Plenty of swimming. We also had to learn how to row. There were whaleboats and cutters, big 32-footers. They took some rowing.'

The focus of the Air Force was on training men. Ohakea airbase was completed in the early months of the war. A flight school was built at Wigram, near Christchurch, and a station at Blenheim, along with airbases at Hobsonville and Whenuapai in west Auckland. Airspeed Oxfords and Harvards were used for advanced flying training; the reliable Tiger Moth was the plane of choice for elementary training. George Judge, who joined the Air Force after his time in the Army, and learnt on both Tiger Moths and Oxfords, thought the former were very good for flying training: 'The Tiger Moth's very forgiving. It's got two wings and plenty of lift.'

By mid-1941 the Air Force had bases and training schools all around the country; the latter were at Whenuapai, New Plymouth, Ohakea, Blenheim, Harewood (Christchurch), Wigram, and Taieri, near Dunedin. During the war, 13,158 trained and semi-trained aircrew passed through the New Zealand air schools. The buildings put up for the 1940 Centennial Exhibition at Rongotai in Wellington were taken over by the Air Force, and the Technical Training School was located at that station, as was the No. 2 Stores Depot. Betty van Praag, one of the first group of WAAFs to be posted to Rongotai, worked in the stores depot and vividly remembers the Exhibition buildings. 'They were huge, they were cold, and they were draughty. The wind whistled through them. We were given a blanket to wrap around ourselves because it was so cold. We had no uniforms, and every hour or so they would muster us outside and we'd walk or run around the building to get warm and then come back to our office desks and wrap our blankets around ourselves. It was very basic.' There was also a recruit training school at Harewood, and an electrical and wireless school, an armament school and an administrative school at Wigram. Many of these were moved to other bases as the war progressed.

HOME DEFENCE

AT THE END OF NOVEMBER 1941, there were 82,000 men in New Zealand's armed forces, 47,000 of whom were serving overseas. In addition, there were 35,000 in the Territorial forces. After Japan entered the war, the whole of the Territorial Force was mobilised in early 1942 to form the basis of the Home Defence Army, which would be New Zealand's main defence should the Japanese invade. At the same time the National Military Reserve was incorporated into the Territorials. By March 1942, there were 65,000 men in this force, married men, as well as single men, being conscripted.

Although invasion was not in fact contemplated by Japan in 1942, people in New Zealand feared that it was going to happen. As Maisie Munro recalled, 'They got close enough to it. Got to Australia.' Harry Spencer remembered that he was waiting for the invasion every day: 'People like myself who didn't know would say, what the heck was going to stop them?'

The Air Force also played its part in the home defence scheme. Air Force operations were run from three group headquarters, based in Auckland, Wellington and Christchurch. New squadrons were formed, including a bomber reconnaissance squadron, which carried out offshore patrols and searches. This was tedious but necessary work. By May 1943, the Air Force had established 16 radar units, which operated around the coast, mainly in the North Island. Their role was to assist the Navy in tracking all

A group of WAAF plotters track ships in association with the Navy, using information from radar units around the coast, 1943. RNZAF Official, via Air Force Museum, Christchurch, PR381

ships; aircraft were sent up to investigate vessels discovered in unexpected positions. The Auckland and New Plymouth stations were also responsible for guiding overseas aircraft — usually American — that needed help in finding their airfield. In September 1943, the RNZAF reached its peak strength in New Zealand, with over 30,000 personnel at 33 stations and depots around the country.

Japanese prisoners of war returning to Featherston POW camp after a day's work. ATL, John Pascoe Collection, F-766-1/4

In August 1943, the Navy established a wireless telegraph station (call sign ZLO) at Waiouru to receive and send secret signal traffic between New Zealand and naval establishments in countries such as Canada, India and the United Kingdom. Japanese signals were also monitored, along with general messages from British warships all around the world. By August 1945, the station had received 7,905,000 messages and sent 9,486,000; it also handled most of the high-priority secret signal traffic in connection with the surrender of Japan for the British Admiralty. Maisie Munro, who worked there as a leading Wren and then a petty officer, recalls that all the messages were received in Morse and sent to the Navy Office in Wellington for decoding.

By 1943, the decrease in the perceived threat of a Japanese invasion — as a result of the Japanese defeats in the naval battles of the Coral Sea and at Midway, and an American counter-offensive in the Solomon Islands (for which New Zealand became a base) — meant that the Home Defence Army could be greatly reduced in size. As George Judge recalls, those over 21 and deemed fit were sent overseas, and those under that age (or unfit for overseas service) were sent back to work or manpowered into essential industries. George returned to his former job at the Department of Maori Affairs in Gisborne. By mid-1943, there were around 33,000 left serving full-time in the Army at home. At the end of December, the Home Guard was placed in reserve and all training was discontinued. Recruiting for WAACs also stopped.

The government had taken responsibility for the control and custody of Japanese prisoners of war captured by US forces in the South Pacific. A POW camp was set up at Featherston in the Wairarapa, and it was here that, in an affray following a stand-off between prisoners and guards in February 1943, the sole New Zealand fatal casualty resulting from enemy action on home soil occurred. A guard was killed and 9 others injured; 48 Japanese were shot dead in the incident.

The only servicemen to be killed in New Zealand waters as a result of enemy action were five sailors who died when a German mine laid in June 1940 blew up their ship, HMS *Puriri*, off Bream Head in Northland in May 1941.

HOME GUARD

ALTHOUGH IT HAS COME to be seen as rather a joke, especially since the British television series *Dad's Army* was screened, the Home Guard allowed men who were too young or too old for the armed forces, or who were in reserved occupations, to feel that they were contributing to the defence of New Zealand, something that became especially important after Japan entered the war. And it was not only a Pakeha group — around 7000 Maori men also served in the Home Guard.

In August 1940, the War Cabinet, a two-party group of ministers, composed of Peter Fraser, Walter Nash, Fred Jones, Dan Sullivan, and Opposition leaders Adam Hamilton and Gordon Coates, approved the establishment of a Home Guard force, under the direction of the National Service Department, to back up the Home Defence Army. There was a Dominion Commander (initially Major-General Robert Young), 3 military district commanders, and 16 area officers who were appointed by the government but nominated by the Returned Soldiers' Association (RSA). Membership was voluntary, unpaid and open to all men aged over 16. As most were in full-time work, the men trained in their spare time, at evenings and weekends. George Clark remembers that his group trained every Saturday at the local Te Pahu hall. They learnt how to use weapons, had shooting practice and signals training, and took part in a number of manoeuvres. They were even provided with lunch.

The Home Guard was supposed to assist the Army by coast-watching in areas that were not

Members of the Home Guard being led through Ngaio, Wellington, by pipers of the Wellington Regiment and Scots College. ATL, Evening Post Collection, PAColl-8557-45

already covered, opposing enemy landings until the Army could arrive, and hindering the movement of enemy forces by constructing obstacles. George Clark remembers that a neighbouring unit had a road block consisting of a large totara log, and his unit built a lookout point which gave good views over the valley where he lived. The Guard was also to help with demolition work and provide guards for internment camps, docks, and radio and cable stations, should there be an invasion.

In 1941, control of the Home Guard was transferred to the Army. It was put on a much more professional footing after the attack on Pearl Harbor, and many groups trained more with Territorial forces and regular troops. In April 1942, the government made Home Guard service compulsory. Seventy thousand men enrolled and around 31,000 were called up for service. It was at this time that the Guard finally got a uniform — previously they had worn an armband. George Clark does not have fond memories of the uniform, which he is convinced dated from the South African War.

By the end of 1943, the Guard was pretty much shut down. There were to be no further parades and uniforms had to be returned to unit commands. George Clark recalls that he was sent an account for 1s 7d because he failed to return a field dressing with his uniform. He refused to pay.

WOMEN'S SERVICE

THE WOMEN'S WAR SERVICE AUXILIARY (WWSA) was established in 1940, and by 1941 was the official organisation responsible for the co-ordination of women's war work. At its peak there were around 75,000 women involved. Janet Fraser, the Prime Minister's wife, headed the organisation's Dominion Council. To begin with, the local branches of the WWSA handled women's applications to the WAAF, the WAAC and the WRNS. Suitable candidates were forwarded to the WWSA headquarters in Wellington, and from there to the appropriate defence force departments. The National Service Department checked that none of the applicants were working in reserved occupations.

Hazel Rowe recalls that her involvement in the WWSA in Christchurch included signals and car maintenance training, and she was also in the local WWSA band. 'We had a drum section and we used to play in front of parades and things. It was a khaki uniform, quite creamy khaki with a peak cap.' Her group of around 50 women trained in Hagley Park in their spare time and even spent some weekends helping to harvest tomatoes at local market gardens. Other activities in which WWSA members were involved included collecting money for patriotic appeals and war bonds, working on telephone switchboards (as Jane McIntyre did in Whangarei

Women's War Service Auxiliary Medical Ambulance Division, New Plymouth. Joan Court-Patience collection

A WAAC puts a roast into the oven. ATL, New Zealand Free Lance Collection, PAColl-8602-40

before she joined the Army), and more traditional women's work, such as knitting comforts for sailors serving overseas.

By 1942, all the branches of the armed forces had accepted women into their ranks. The Women's Auxiliary Air Force was the first to be established, in January 1941, followed by the Women's Auxiliary Army Corps at the end of that year. The Navy began accepting Wrens at the end of May 1942; the first intake consisted of women who were to be trained as telegraphists, including Maisie Munro, whose story appears in this book. They initially worked as clerks, cooks, waitresses, kitchen hands and nurses. Maisie Takle was a VAD nurse in the Air Force, while Kath Dyall worked as a waitress in the Army, as did Heather Crispe in the Navy. As time went by, the occupations broadened: women like Ngaire Gibbons became drivers, and Gwen Stevens worked in the radar filter room, tracking the arrival of aircraft in New Zealand airspace. Some in the Air Force became expert repairers of aircraft. Peter Crispe recalls WAAFs mending tiny tears in the wings of Tiger Moths when he was stationed at Rukuhia, near Hamilton.

The initial reason for enlisting women was to release men to serve overseas. The Navy, for example, spent some time discussing whether or not their proposed women's force would be permitted to work at night. If they could, they would be able to replace male telegraphists and signals ratings, who could then be sent overseas. Some of the women were not received with open arms by the men with whom they had to work. Maisie Munro recalls that the men at wireless station ZLP on Tinakori Hill in Wellington were 'a bit doubtful' about the Wrens who came to be telegraphists. 'One person in particular was really bad. He was sarcastic to us and it was really quite difficult to cope with.' Betty van Praag, on the other hand, recalls that the WAAFs at Rongotai were greeted with pleasure, along with some good-natured teasing.

The first WAAF Superintendent was Frances Kain, who served from 1941 until 1943, when she was succeeded by Elsie Carlyon. Two hundred WAAFs began work at Rongotai airbase in April 1941.

Among them was Betty van Praag, who recalls, 'We had no numbers, we had no uniform, we didn't have anything. We were sent to Rongotai. There I went and was mustered into the equipment section. Shorthand and typing, working in the office. I was secretary to the adjutant of the equipment section.' Betty lived at home, but those who came from other places in New Zealand were sent to private hotels. Eventually, accommodation, or a Waafery as it was called, was built at Rongotai. Maisie Takle recalls that this consisted of prefabricated units, with each room housing 10 young women. She enjoyed the experience, saying that, 'There was always something going on. Lighting the gas fire and making toast at it by night, that sort of thing. It was good fun.' By the time the war ended, WAAFs had served at stations from Taieri in the south to Whenuapai and Hobsonville in the north, with 20 being sent to Fiji in January 1943 and 9 to Norfolk Island. WAAFs also served in New Caledonia.

A member of the Women's Land Service with a herd of cows, Rotorua, 1943. ATL, John Pascoe Collection, F-544-1/4

Vida Jowett was the Chief Commander of the WAAC, based in Wellington, and was responsible for the largest group of the women's armed services. At their peak strength, there were 4600 in the WAAC, 3700 in the WAAF and 700 in the WRNS. A significant number of WAACs served overseas, in the Middle East and the Pacific.

In New Zealand, they performed a range of duties, many outside the initial constrained list of occupations for women. Ngaire Gibbons was a driver responsible for transporting trucks from Petone and Porirua over the Rimutaka Hill to a truck park at Tauherenikau racecourse in the Wairarapa, and often up to Waiouru. Hazel Rowe worked in one of the heavy anti-aircraft batteries based around the coast

A poster parade for peace in Wellington, c. 1940. ATL, F-152943-1/2

— she was stationed at Mt Pleasant, near Lyttelton. Her job was on the predictors, which calculated an aircraft's flight path so that the gunners had a better chance of shooting it down.

The WRNS was established in April 1942, with Ruth Herrick as the director of Wrens and Helen Fenwick as her deputy. Herrick had had administrative experience as Commissioner in the Girl Guides movement, and Fenwick, now Helen Phibbs, recalls her as having a stern expression but a very good sense of humour. To begin with, both women personally interviewed each Wren applicant. Helen Phibbs recalls that they were looking for young women who were 'steady', could tolerate discipline, and would accept any job to which they were directed once they had enlisted. The other women's forces, while larger and therefore with a less personal recruitment style, sought applicants with similar attributes.

In October 1942, the WAAC was formally constituted as part of the Army, meaning that women had equivalent ranks to men in similar roles. When the WAAF became part of the RNZAF in the same year, as well as being granted equivalent ranks to the men, women were also promoted in the same way.

New Zealand women also served in uniform, but as civilians, as what were popularly termed 'land girls'. The Women's Land Corps was established in November 1941 under the auspices of the WWSA, but in September 1942 it was reconstituted as the Women's Land Service. Pay and conditions improved and a proper uniform was introduced. It was a voluntary scheme until March 1944, when women began to be assigned to farms by District Manpower Offices. Recruitment ended in August 1945 and the Service was disbanded at the end of April 1946.

CONSCIENTIOUS OBJECTORS

AS MENTIONED ABOVE, there was a strong feeling amongst many New Zealanders that it was their duty to fight for King and country. Despite that, not everybody was prepared to take part in the war. Merv Browne, whose story appears in this book, was a pacifist and decided that he could not participate in the killing of people. When conscription was introduced in 1940, he became a conscientious objector and was eventually detained for the duration of the war — or, in his case, until May 1946. Not all refused to serve — some became part of non-combatant units, such as field ambulances — because, while they were

not prepared to take arms, they felt that they must act to defeat fascist Germany and Italy. The number of dissenters was very small, but their story is an important part of the history of the war in New Zealand.

Some of the Protestant churches in New Zealand, such as the Methodists and Presbyterians, had expressed their opposition to war in the years after the First World War, generally as a reaction to the huge loss of life between 1914 and 1918. Once war was declared in 1939, however, splits began to appear between those church members who believed that even in wartime Christians should oppose war, and the majority, who felt that the war was a *fait accompli* and, it could be argued, a just war against the fascist powers of Germany and Italy. Some of the smaller religious groups, such as the Society of Friends (Quakers) and Assemblies of God, had long been pacifist and had also been conscientious objectors during the First World War.

Other people and groups opposed war, or this war, for reasons to do with politics and humanitarianism. Some were socialist, others believed in internationalism and especially in the role of the League of Nations in preventing wars through arbitration and economic sanctions. The inability of the League to prevent international conflict, however, tested the faith of those who believed in arbitration. Many of those who argued that capitalism caused wars changed their positions once the Soviet Union joined the Allies in the

war against Germany in 1941.

After war was declared in September 1939, members of the two most prominent anti-war organisations in New Zealand, the Peace Pledge Union and the Christian Pacifist Society, spoke at open-air meetings in Wellington's Pigeon (now Te Aro) Park, and also in other centres. They were usually arrested for obstructing police, on the grounds that as the meetings might turn violent, the police were justified in preventing them. The open-air meetings were held regularly to begin with, but after a while most of the speakers had been arrested or conscripted into the armed forces and then sent to detention camps for refusing to serve. The meetings continued sporadically during the war, and Merv Browne recalls his relief when he was arrested while speaking in Pigeon Park in 1944 after escaping from his detention camp. 'I'd never spoken publicly before.' It was not long before he was arrested, he says; 'as a matter of fact, it wasn't soon enough for me. I'd run out of things to say.'

Conscription regulations provided for the establishment of Armed Forces Appeal Boards to deal with appeals against overseas service on grounds of conscience, hardship, public interest or status, and appeals on grounds of conscience against Territorial service. It was generally felt that unless it was made difficult to win an appeal, many men might feel that they opposed war on this ground, which would make fighting the war almost impossible. In the event, fewer than 2 per cent of the men called up lodged appeals on grounds of conscience.

Given this climate of opinion, it was often difficult to convince an appeal board that you truly objected to war. Applicants had to show that they believed it was wrong to engage in war under any circumstances. Many, like Merv, did not bother to appeal. A friend of his had lost his appeal and he recalls thinking, 'I can't imagine anyone more sincere than Jack. I'm not going to go through with it, so I notified them that I wouldn't be applying for a dispensation.' Under regulations issued in August 1940, men who refused service had to appear before a magistrate, who either sentenced them to a jail term followed by detention, or sent them straight to a detention camp for the duration of the war.

Detention camps for conscientious objectors who refused to serve in the armed forces began to be

Crowds listen to the RNZAF Band, VJ Day, Wellington. ATL, John Pascoe Collection, PAColl-5926-49

established in October 1941. The first was at Strathmore, near Reporoa in the middle of the North Island. By the end of the war 13 detention camps and sub-camps housed 803 defaulters who had refused to enter the armed forces. The men undertook farm or forestry work, flax cultivation and other agricultural pursuits.

Discipline at the camps was strict. There were roll calls, no leave, and pay depended on good behaviour; visitors and mail were limited, and the latter was censored. Refusal to obey an order attracted penalties, ranging from solitary confinement on a diet of bread and water, to terms in jail. Merv Browne received all these punishments at various times during his incarceration. It could be argued that the government was doing its best with what it saw as obstinate and unruly — and articulate — men, whom many felt should not have a more comfortable existence than that of servicemen overseas. It could also be said that it was an unnecessarily harsh regime, much harsher than those in Britain and other Commonwealth countries. The government argued that the harshness deterred others; the conscientious objectors and their supporters said that they would be happy to do useful work in the community. It was a difficult situation for both sides. The government, some of whose members — such as Walter Nash — were quite sympathetic, had to consider the arguments of newspaper editorials and organisations such as the RSA, which suggested that the men were being treated far better than they should be. Pacifists thought that they should not be punished for their beliefs when others — members of some religious groups — were given dispensation on the grounds of their objection to war.

By the end of 1945, around 300 conscientious objectors had been released from detention, and in April 1946 about 150 remained in camps or prison. The RSA persisted in its calls for further punishment, stating that conscientious objectors should be detained for 12 months after the end of the war, barred from employment in the public service, and have their civil rights (the vote) taken away for 10 years. By the end of June, all had been released — with none of those conditions attached.

THE END OF THE WAR

THE WAR IN EUROPE came to an end when Germany surrendered on 7 May 1945. The news was not unexpected; in fact, victory celebrations in New Zealand had been planned for weeks. VE Day, as it was called, was celebrated in New Zealand on 8 and 9 May. The official announcement was to be made simultaneously in London, Washington and Moscow on 8 May, but was released earlier so it could be published in morning newspapers here on that day. As a result, there were many displays of jubilation. The victory was celebrated on 9 May, too, because the New Zealand authorities wanted to co-ordinate the official celebrations with those held in Britain, where it was still the 8th. It was wonderful news, although the excitement in New Zealand was somewhat muted by the knowledge that there was still Japan to defeat.

At the beginning of August 1945, after Japan had rejected surrender terms offered by Britain, the United States and China, Prime Minister Peter Fraser made public the government's commitment to fighting the war to the finish. New Zealand forces overseas would be cut from nearly 58,000 to 29,000, and the forces at home from 42,000 to 26,000. A division of around 16,000 men would be the country's contribution to the Commonwealth force that would take part in the invasion of Japan. The use of atomic bombs on 6 and 9 August soon made these arrangements irrelevant, although New Zealand did later send a sizable force to assist with the occupation of Japan.

Many of the people interviewed for this book have strong memories of VJ Day, 15 August 1945. Maisie Takle recalls roaring around the airbase at Hobsonville on ambulances and fire engines with the sirens shrieking. Derek Laver says that it was a 'wild and woolly night' in Auckland — 'the whole of Queen Street seemed to be full of people dancing and singing, carrying on'. It was, as Fraser put it, the end of six 'long, anxious, worrying, dangerous, tragic years'.

By the end of August, there were 15,619 people in the Army in New Zealand and demobilisation was proceeding apace. The demobilisation of the home forces was done in an order of priority, whereby men and women who had formerly worked in such fields as agriculture and building were sent home first. As Hazel Rowe attests, women who wanted to marry were also allowed to leave quickly. Between VJ Day and the end of March 1946, 73,894 men and 3360 women were demobilised.

After the war, Finance Minister Walter Nash reported that it had cost the country £640 million, not counting pensions, rehabilitation costs and future interest on loans. He added that the rehabilitation scheme was intended to restore to ex-servicemen and women the opportunities that they had missed out on because of their war service. Priorities for the scheme were the provision of state houses and building materials, and education and trade-training facilities. As Kath Dyall and others recalled, the 'rehab' loans were used for buying sections and building and furnishing houses. Loans for furniture and tools were interest-free; those for businesses were made at an interest rate of 4 per cent, and those for land at 3 per cent. Maisie Munro recalls that 50 per cent of allocations of state houses and flats were made to ex-servicemen.

Chas Woodley, who lost both eyes and his right hand, is taught to operate a small loom in Auckland after the war. Archives New Zealand/Te Rua Mahara o te Kawanatanga, Wellington Office [ATL, 16835-1/4 (AAQT6401, A9619)]

The rehabilitation scheme had got under way during the war as returned servicemen came home either because they were deemed to have served long enough or because of injury. In October 1941, the Rehabilitation Act was passed. It provided for a council to advise the government on work training for returned service personnel, and for loans to establish houses, farms and businesses. A Rehabilitation Board was set up to handle the practical details of the scheme, such as arranging employment. By 1951 there were 112 local advisory committees, although the number of these fell quickly as their work was completed, and by 1955 there were only 9 left. It was fortunate for the board and its committees that there was no shortage of work in the country at the time.

As well as trade training — primarily in trades connected with house construction to begin with, as there was an acute need for more adequate housing — the rehabilitation scheme also provided for university education and teacher training. It was an extraordinary opportunity for many young people who had been unable to have the education they would have liked because of the effects of the Depression of the 1930s. The war gave Maisie Takle the opportunity to train as a nurse, and, after the war ended, the rehabilitation scheme enabled people who had perhaps worked in shops or as clerks to go to university and become lawyers or doctors.

Peacetime was not wonderful for everyone, of course. Some men suffered from psychological trauma and many had been physically maimed, which denied them many avenues of employment. Even those who were not badly enough affected to have treatment found it difficult to settle back into everyday life. It was not easy for those they returned to, either. They had to resume life with people they had not seen for many years, and who had often been through experiences which they could not or did not wish to share with their loved ones.

It might be thought that those who served at home would find the resumption of civilian life less difficult, as their family ties had not been so completely severed. Harry Spencer recalls, however, that after he was demobilised from the Army, he and his wife and twin boys had to live in a small flat in the Wellington suburb of Khandallah, because nothing else was available. 'They were pretty hard times . . . I was used to a big crowd of men around me all the time, and then to come home to a quiet house with the family . . . I was very easily upset.' It was difficult at work, too, compared to the Army, where he had been used to having some authority. 'In there, I was one of the boys, and when I came out into civvy life it was completely different. It took me such a long time to adapt to being told by one of my fellow workmates what to do.'

REFLECTIONS

WHEN ASKED TO REFLECT upon their time in the armed forces, all of the people in this book responded that they had grown up emotionally during the war years. Most of the women explained that, as it was the first time they had been away from home, they learnt to be more independent, even though they were in situations where they were subject to much discipline. In the Air Force, Peter Crispe met the man who was to teach him to be a watchmaker, a profession he loved from the beginning and still enjoys in retirement, saying that 'there was never a moment when I hated what I was doing or felt unhappy with life. I've been so lucky in that respect.' Derek Laver and Harry Spencer were sad that they did not serve overseas, and Derek recalls that after the war people were quite disparaging when they heard that he had served in home waters. 'It hurt like hell, because every man-jack of us felt the same — would have loved to have gone overseas. It wasn't our choice.' In the next breath he added that he had no regrets about enlisting and had enjoyed being in the Navy.

Many of them also have interesting opinions about war in general. Derek Laver again: 'Why we can't get on and live peacefully together, I'll never know. When you're young, it's a great adventure. When you're old and look back on it, you think, How bloody stupid.' And Betty van Praag brings her experiences as a mother to her opinion: 'Now that I have a son, [war] seems a total, utter, endless obscenity. Nobody wins. Nobody.'

FURTHER READING

The war in New Zealand is covered by Nancy M. Taylor's *The Home Front* (two volumes, 1986), an excellent source for readers seeking more information on any of the events or organisations mentioned in passing in the introduction. A general account of this country and the Second World War, although with limited coverage of the war at home, is Ian McGibbon's *New Zealand and the Second World War* (2003). This is useful too on US troops in New Zealand and the progress of the war in the Pacific. J.M.S. Ross covers the Air Force at home in *Royal New Zealand Air Force* (1955). *The Oxford Companion to New Zealand Military History* (2000) has useful entries on aspects of the war in New Zealand.

Books dealing with the women's services include: Grant Howard's *Happy in the Service: An Illustrated History of the Women's Royal New Zealand Naval Service 1942–1977* (1985); Iris Latham's compilation *The WAAC Story: The Story of the New Zealand Womens'* [sic] *Army Auxiliary Corps* (1986); and Bathia McKenzie's *The WAAF Book: A Scrapbook of Wartime Memories* (1982). Bee Dawson's edited interviews with WAAFs were published as *Spreading Their Wings* (2004).

Dianne Bardsley's *The Land Girls* (2000) covers women who worked in the Women's Land Service, and David Grant gives a good background on those who were pacifists and conscientious objectors during the war in *Out in the Cold* (1986). Deborah Montgomerie's *The Women's War: New Zealand Women 1939–45* (2001) is a study of women's experiences, both civilian and military. Judith Fyfe's *War Stories Our Mothers Never Told Us* (1995), Eve Ebbett's *When the Boys Were Away* (1984), Lauris Edmond's *Women in Wartime* (1986), and Jim Sullivan's *Doing Our Bit* (2002) are personal accounts of women's activities in New Zealand during the war.

Harry Bioletti's *The Yanks Are Coming: The American Invasion of New Zealand 1942–1944* (1989) and Jock Phillips' *Brief Encounter: American Forces and the New Zealand People 1942–1945* (1992) are social histories of the US troops' time in this country.

'MY LIFE HAD CHANGED'

Jane McIntyre, w812175, Corporal, WAAC

Jane Bristow (Ngapuhi) was born in the East Coast township of Te Araroa in 1921. Her parents, Alfred (Te Hawhe) and Annie Bristow, farmed there, but returned to family land near Kawakawa in Northland when Jane was a child. Jane was one of nine children. After leaving school, she worked in Whangarei as a housekeeper. Through a friend of her father, she volunteered as a weekend switchboard operator for the Army after war was declared in 1939. Jane joined the Women's War Service Auxiliary in Whangarei and did volunteer work for the YMCA, opening the hall on Sunday afternoons so that men in camp at Kensington could use the facilities.

MY FATHER'S FRIEND suggested I enlist and get paid for what I was doing. Then I enlisted. That was in 1942. I understood that once you went into the Army you were cut off from your family, so I thought, I'll have six weeks off before I'm due to go to the Army. During that six weeks I got really ill. I sat on damp grass and eventually I got pleurisy. I ended up in hospital. I wrote and told the Army that I was sick and they said to write to them when I was feeling better. It was the end of 1942 when I wrote and told them I was well enough, but because it was close to Christmas, I wasn't called up till 6 January 1943.

Mum and Dad were so protective — to think I was going to Auckland all by myself. Every now and again they'd tell me, 'You've got to look after yourself in Queen Street. It's a terrible place. You've got to hold on to your money.' All this sort of thing. I knew I'd be all right, so I just let them haul out all these bits of advice to me: 'Don't forget to say your prayers.'

The morning came for me to go to Auckland, and my mother came on the bus with me. The last thing she said to me as I boarded the train in Kawakawa was 'Hang on to your money.' I thought, What money? I've got hardly any money.

Previous page: *Chief Commander Vida Jowett inspects her WAACs.* ATL, W.H. Raine Collection, G-20866-1/4
Above: *Private Jane Bristow.* Jane McIntyre collection

A very different YMCA from the one Jane Bristow worked in at Whangarei.
This one is in North Africa. ATL, Steptoe Collection, F-140074-1/2

When you told your mother and your father that you were going to join the Army, what did they say?
Besides being concerned for me, I think in their own way they were pleased that I was going to be doing something for King and country. But they wanted to make sure that I was going to be all right.

I got on the train at Kawakawa. We went to all the country places that had no real roads, and at these stations I always had a good look at the people who came to meet the train. The farmers were there in their old woollen shirts. Some of them had a sledge, which was just two wooden runners with bars across — where they put their cream cans — and a horse to pull it along. They always had a cheeky word to the guard. Every station was different. They were just so interesting, it was lovely to see them. I thought I wouldn't see them again for a long, long time, because when anybody talked about the Army . . . well, some of my mother's friends said, 'You'll be running around a parade ground with a heavy backpack on your back all day,' and things like that. I thought it'd be a long time before I'd get home to see my folks again.

It didn't put you off when people told you that?
No. No, I thought, I'm prepared to take it. I thought, It's for King and country. I've got to do my share. My war effort.

Only one of Jane's other siblings joined the armed forces. Her older brother joined the Army, but did not go overseas because he was married.

Later on, when I was in Papakura Camp, we had a lecture about not saluting the officers. I was going down to the station one day and who should I meet coming up into camp but my brother, who was an officer. I had to salute him because our commanding officer, I knew, was a few hundred yards behind me. I threw him this salute and I said, 'You wouldn't get this if she wasn't behind me.' He grinned.

What was it like arriving at Auckland?

Auckland Railway Station, c. 1936.
ATL, A.P. Godber Collection,
F-20324-1/2

Army band in front of church huts at Trentham camp. ATL, S.C. Smith Collection, G-48408-1/2

I got out of the train and looked and I thought, What a long platform, what a lot of people. Coming from the country, being green, not being used to a lot of people, I just couldn't take it all in. Then I heard my mother's advice ringing in my ears: 'Don't stand and gape', so I thought I'd better get moving, but I didn't know where I was going, because all I knew was to go to Auckland and I would be met there. I thought I'd better look for somebody who might be looking for me. I joined in the flow of people and came up into this brightly lit railway station. Everybody was buzzing around, all the activity was too much. I thought, What am I doing here?

There are big pillars at the station, so I thought I'd better stand with my back to a pillar and watch the entrance. I could watch the people coming from the train and I could watch the people scurrying out and catching the trams. I had a good view. I'd had some military training, so I stood at ease, my little suitcase in front of me, and I kept watching everybody's faces, hoping somebody would come along to claim me. I stood there for — it seemed like hours. Eventually a smartly uniformed WAAC came along with about five other civilian girls in tow. She said, 'Jane Bristow?' I said, 'Yes.' She said, 'Thank goodness for that. Come on, we've got a train to catch.' She hurried us back onto the platform and said, 'We're going to Papakura.' That was the first time I knew where I was going.

There were five of us, and Jean Lowry was the corporal who met us at the station. I admired her, she was so young and attractive and smart. We got off the train, each of us carrying our little suitcase. We had to cross over an overhead walkway. We went down the other side, and, as we went through the turnstiles, she said, 'We're now in Papakura Military Camp.' There were pines growing along on the right and I could smell their scent. It was a long, long walk up into camp. Then I saw all these green camouflaged huts. It was about tea time and there were only one or two soldiers around. They gave us wolf whistles as we passed.

On the way up, Jean Lowry told us the rules. She said, 'These huts are strictly out of bounds. God help you if you cross the boundary.' There was a Catholic recreation hut, a Church of England hut, a YMCA hut and then the Salvation Army hut. Then you crossed over and there was the canteen where Jean said later we could do our shopping. She said, 'You're now in B Block.' And that was going to be our home.

Jean told us to leave our luggage on the veranda. We were to be interviewed, one at a time. My turn came. I went in; there was a very tall woman sitting at the table. She looked so military, sort of forbidding. She was flanked by two younger women, neatly dressed in khaki, with shiny brass buttons. She was Miss Hawkins. She took down our names and we were all given a number, and I remember my number was 812175. After over 60 years I can still remember it. We were told we were to be known more or less by the number. I entered the orderly room as Miss Jane Bristow, and I came out as Bristow, E.J., WAAC, 812175. Private Bristow. My life had changed.

Can you remember how you felt? Were you excited, or worried?
No, just curious, accepting everything. My mother was strict, so we were used to discipline, used to being told what to do, and knew how to be obedient. I knew that's what I had enlisted for.

When we had all been interviewed, Jean Lowry showed us where we were to stay. It was in Hut 4. It had big double doors, and concrete steps. We stood on the steps, looking in. It was so bare — no mats on the floor, just wooden boards, little wooden beds. We went in and chose our beds, and one of the girls said, 'To think I left the comforts of home to come to this!' Jean Lowry came to take us to the quartermaster's store for our bedding. Me, being the slowest, the shyest, I was the last one. While I was in the queue I watched the girls signing for their palliasse, which was a straw mattress with thick ticking, their sheets, their towel and everything. When it came to my turn, being the last, they could not find a palliasse. The people in the quartermaster's store said they'd looked everywhere, they couldn't find a palliasse, there was nothing more they could do, they couldn't help me. I signed for what I was issued with

Soldiers bring gear out of a hut, Papakura camp. ATL, PAColl-8847

and got back to the hut. The girls were busy making their beds and I said, 'I haven't got a mattress.'

I looked at those hard wooden slats and thought, Am I going to spend my first night on those hard boards? Then I thought, Oh well, I've been travelling all day — because it was now early evening — maybe I'll be tired enough to sleep anywhere. One of the girls said, 'Miss Hawkins said she was there to help us at any time.' Just then she passed the door. My feet took on wings and I was out that door as quick as anything, and I told her my sad story. She looked at me — she had beautiful warm eyes, I knew I was going to like her — and said, 'Come with me.' She took me to, I think it was Hut 1, threw open a door and said, 'There. You can sleep there.' It was one of the sergeants' rooms with a nice big fat kapok mattress. I could have hugged her! I thanked her, I think, a thousand times.

I wrote to my mother that night, as promised, and told her everything. Told her I was quite safe, and I was sure I would be all right, that they had nothing to worry about.

I slept like a log. Too right I did. I was tired. It had been an all-day journey. The first thing in the morning I was lying awake — I must have been just awake — and I heard these footsteps coming up the hut, then a big loud voice saying: 'Wakey, wakey everybody. Feet on the floor!' I sprang out of bed, grabbed my dressing gown, went over to the ablution block, had a quick wash, cleaned my teeth and came back to my room. The ablution block had a cold concrete floor with a couple of showers and concrete tubs.

Jane (right) returning from the ablution block with her friend Bonnie Cairns.
Jane McIntyre collection

Then it was breakfast time. We had army porridge. I'd heard about army porridge, but I was grateful because I didn't have to cook it. You could hear remarks from a lot of the girls from the well-to-do homes. After breakfast, the whistle blew, we went out and we had to go and pick up all the rubbish around our block. Every little matchstick or piece of paper. That was called 'emu parade'. That was before breakfast, actually. Every morning.

When the whistle blew, you knew you had to get out and line up somewhere. For meal times it was at the end of the huts; otherwise it was on the parade ground, which was by the orderly room. It was a big parade ground. It was funny watching some girls who could not march. They'd put their right hand and their right foot forward at the same time. The poor instructors. We did a lot of that in our six weeks' initial training.

I think the first day was spent on lectures and injections.

Were there any other young Maori women there?

There would have been one or two sitting at the dining table, but I didn't really get to know them because the Hut 4 girls stayed together, so we didn't get to know many people.

Each day we had to go to the ante-room to look up the routine orders, which told us what was happening that day. The routine orders were always pinned up on the noticeboard. At one of our first lectures, Miss Hawkins had said that every day one girl had to go and polish her buttons, be her batwoman for the day. We'd been there a couple of weeks when one of the girls said my name was in the routine orders to do batwoman duty. I'd asked the girls before what they did. They said it was a good, easy day. They loved it.

So on Monday morning I went over, clip clop through this big, empty, cold building which was the officers' kitchens. There was a brown enamel electric jug on the bench, so I filled it up, boiled the kettle and made the tea. Miss Hawkins had her tea at six o'clock in the morning, so I took it across. I stood in front of her bedroom door and it was six o'clock. I was right on time. I knocked on the door and she said, 'Come in.'

I went in and there she was, tall, stately Miss Hawkins, sitting bolt upright against her headboard. She looked very military. She was sitting as if she was sitting to attention. She had striped pyjamas, and I thought they were the sort of pyjamas my dad wore. Her wispy grey hair was curled up in pipe curlers, and she looked so comical. I wanted to burst out laughing, but instead I must have just stood there and gaped. She said, 'Come in, girl, don't stand there.' I took the tea over to her, and she told me to take her jacket down and her shoes, and as I went out the door she said, 'And don't get polish on my uniform. Use the button stick.' 'Yes, ma'am.' And off I went.

When I came back from polishing them, she said, 'Bristow, that was my first hot cup of tea.' I felt sorry for her and I thought, You can't run an army on cold tea. I was very pleased that on my way over I had put the saucer on top of the cup and kept the tea hot for her. Anyway, she said after breakfast to go back and do her room, and later, while I was doing her room, she asked me would I do it for the rest of the week. I thought it'd be a nice, easy week, so I said I would do it, because it was no trouble to take her a hot cup of tea, no trouble at all. Before the week was up, she asked me if I would do it full-time. I said, 'But ma'am, I'm doing my signals training.' She said it would be quite a long time before they had a signal corps going, and she dangled a carrot in front of the donkey by saying, 'No emu parade, you know. You'll answer to no one but me.' I thought, I won't have to take orders from any sergeants. I just have to obey her. Nobody can tell me what to do. That's the impression she gave me, so I said I would do it. She was such a lovely, warm, caring mother. She really was a lovely person.

Did you stay in Hut 4?
No, we only stayed there till our six weeks' training was up, and because I was batwoman to our officer commanding, I was put on staff into Hut 1A.

I wasn't always just batwoman. Later on, when Sister Ritchie came and she needed a holiday, they got me to look after the RAP room for her. I thought, I can't do it. I'm not a nurse. I asked her what I had to do, and she said just attend the RAP room, which is Regimental Aid Post, but I called it the 'repair

*Jane (right) eating Christmas dinner
at Papakura camp, 1943.*
Jane McIntyre collection

room'. She said the girls signed for their sanitary pads every time they were issued, and to dish out aspirins for anyone with headaches and things like that. And she said, 'The hospital's just down the road. You can ring the hospital any time.' I did that for a week. But, oh golly, did I count the days till she came back.

Was that because you could fit it in around being a batwoman?
Yes. Eventually a nurse came in to help Sister Ritchie, but in the meantime I took over. When the librarian had leave, I was librarian for a week.

Later on, we had Third Div officers who had come back from the Islands, and quite a lot of them were pretty yellow-looking. Miss Hardcastle said, 'I've got a new job for you.' The Third Div officers were coming into camp and I would be required in the dining room. I said, 'I'm no waitress. I'll probably spill soup down their back.' She said I wouldn't need to do that, I'd be a sort of a maître d'. She said, 'I'll give you five of the best waitresses.' I was the first one there, last one to leave, but I had very little to do because the waitresses were so good.

Jane recalls getting the WAAC uniform piece by piece.

The first thing they issued us with were thick lisle stockings, and then I think they gave us shoes. Some of the girls went on leave wearing these thick stockings — and it would be summertime — and their shoes, and greatcoats. They put their greatcoats over their silk clothes or their print dresses, or whatever they were wearing, and they said it was agony wearing that greatcoat buttoned up because they were so embarrassed. Eventually we got issued with smocks, neat smocks, and we wore them on leave. Then we were all put onto trucks and taken up to a place on Karangahape Road, and we all had made-to-measure glamour suits. It was beautiful serge. Officers' material. Beautiful material. When we went to collect our suits, we couldn't go on leave quick enough to show off our glamour suits.

We had a little glengarry hat. We were issued with that first, and then later I think they gave us the wide-brimmed hats, and then last of all the berets. I didn't like the berets. I thought I looked funny in a beret and I kept my glengarry hat. They were easy, they stayed on in the wind. They were better than the wide-brimmed hats. You just perched them on your head and they stayed there.

Tell me a bit about Miss Hardcastle.
When Miss Hardcastle first came into camp there were funny stories about her because she'd served up in the Islands. She was our last commanding officer. She was tough-looking. She was as rough as anything on the outside, but inside she had a heart of gold. She really was lovely. She and I understood each other, but we didn't have that warmth that I had had with Dorothy Hawkins, our first officer. Dorothy Hawkins was only there for a little while, then she had to go into Auckland to the main establishment there.

After Dorothy Hawkins, the next WAAC CO at Papakura was Mary Geddes.

She always wanted to feel proud of her girls. Your hair had to be an inch above the collar. When we had inspection parade before we went on leave, if there was a little bit of hair hanging on your collar, you were asked to pin it up before going any further. She must have noticed some untidy tresses somewhere, and the first girl she saw with longish hair, she hauled her along to the hairdressers, got the scissors and cut her hair. We never, ever forgot that.

Jane usually managed to stay out of trouble, but was once caught wearing civilian clothes when she went to a Christmas party held by the Motor Transport workshop boys in Takanini. She had made a red pinafore dress and lace blouse at the Army's handicraft hut, and decided she would wear them to the party, although she should have been in uniform. She managed to get out of camp in her party clothes, but got caught on her return.

I put on this offending outfit, then put on my greatcoat and cap. You were properly dressed with your greatcoat and cap. The only trouble with wearing civilian clothes was that you had to wear your khaki stockings and your Army shoes. But never mind, we were colourful. I came back with a girl called Pat. We walked back to camp, and I know somebody had put a red carnation in my hair. It was a great dance. I remember entering camp with my cap twirling around in my fingers. Pat said, 'We'll go round the other side of the hut', but I said, 'No. That's right under Hardy's window. We'll wake her up. We'll go this side.' Then out of the fog loomed this figure. It was Miss Hardcastle with a torch. She couldn't believe it was me she was looking at. I think she thought I could do no wrong. Her mouth flew open. I quickly pulled my greatcoat together to hide the offending outfit. On and on she went. Eventually she said to Pat and I, 'You can go over there. Wait with the rest of them.' We both dodged around her and left her there. When I entered the ante-room there were lots of other people there. One of the CB veterans, she'd been on CB so many times it didn't matter to her, she came in a lot later, looked at us and said, 'Ho, ho, ho. Got some big fish tonight!'

None of us felt that we'd done wrong. It was all good fun till Hardy came in. She came in and she lectured us. I didn't mind being lectured, but then she came and stood in front of me and she seemed to be just lecturing me. She took a step back, looked at everyone, and said, 'You can all scrub huts for a week. You're confined to barracks.' I thought, OK, I'm not on my own. I've got all these mates with me.

The week passed.

It was Sunday, the last day of our CB. Being confined to barracks during the week was no trouble. You just had your tea and went to bed. You couldn't go to the canteen, you couldn't go and socialise with the men down in the recreation huts. We just went to bed, read books, or sat around talking. It was no hardship. But boy, come the weekend . . . I saw a group of CB girls sitting around in a ring on the lawn, so I went and sat beside them and they said the huts were clean. They couldn't scrub them any more. The floors were as white as could be. One of them eventually said they'd like to go for a swim.

*These WAACS are not confined to barracks, but enjoying themselves off duty,
Godley Head, 1943.* ATL, John Pascoe Collection, F-129-1/4

Then everybody thought it'd be wonderful to go for a swim.

> *The women weren't allowed to go to the pool as they were still confined to barracks. Eventually they
> persuaded Jane, who was still Miss Hardcastle's batwoman, to go and plead on their behalf. She
> was successful, and so they not only had their swim but their CB term was slightly shortened.*

When did you leave the Army?
I left after peace was declared. Bonnie, who was my best friend there, her husband came back and so
she went out. One by one the girls started leaving because their boyfriends had come back. I thought
with Bonnie not there I was going to get out.

> *Jane left in 1946 and married George McIntyre in 1949. She had known George, a farmer in
> the area where she grew up, since she was a girl. The couple had six sons and one daughter.
> Jane died in April 2006 after a short illness.*

'CHIEF STOREMAN
IN THE STORES'

Harry SPENCER, 37429,
Staff Sergeant, Supply & Transport

Harry Spencer was born in 1910 at Nar Nar Goon in Gippsland, Victoria. His father, John, had been born in Hokitika, so in the 1930s Harry decided to travel to New Zealand. He had an uncle in Hastings and worked at his service station for a while. Harry then decided he would prefer a different job.

I GOT A JOB driving a baker's cart for Findlay's in Hastings. I'd never harnessed a horse in my life. The boss came out and told me, 'There's your horse, there's the harness. Get cracking.' I said, 'OK.' I brought the horse up. It wouldn't go where I wanted it to go, and I looked across and there were about six jokers splitting themselves laughing, looking through the door at me harnessing this horse. I had the harness back to front, and they came out and harnessed the horse for me.

I must tell you about my first day out. I had a chappie come out with me for two or three days to show me the run. Then the big day came and I did the run on my own. I left the bakehouse about eight o'clock in the morning. The baker's cart was sort of a square box with doors at the back. I got to my third or fourth house, and in those days you used to put your bread in a basket and take it round to the lady's back door. Which I did. When I came back my old horse was missing. It had gone. I dropped the basket on the front lawn and tore round one block after another until I just couldn't go any longer, so I had no other option then but to ask the lady if I could use the phone, and ring up my boss. 'Sorry, Mr Scott, but I've lost my horse and cart.' He couldn't stop laughing. He said, 'You'd better come back to the bakehouse, because it's arrived back down here.'

Harry worked for Findlay's until war was declared in 1939.

Previous page: *Trentham camp, Upper Hutt.* ATL, J. Young Collection, F-49277-1/2
Above: *Harry Spencer.* Harry Spencer collection

Marching to the Hastings railway station en route to Trentham camp, 1940. Harry Spencer collection

After giving it lots and lots of thought, I decided I'd like to join the Army and I went and told my boss. He was quite agreeable. He said, 'Your job will be here for you when you come back.' So I joined up and I was called in for the Fourth Echelon. I remember marching down to the Hastings drill hall about four o'clock in the afternoon. There was quite a crowd to see us off. We had some hard cases on the train. Everybody was a little bit serious. We left Hastings at four o'clock, arriving at Trentham railway station around about midnight. One little bloke, I think his name was Eric Ludlow, an ex-jockey, all he had in the world was a pair of socks wrapped round his neck. He told the commanding officer that he had a suitcase and he'd lost it. They spent quite some half an hour, easily, hanging around in the railway station looking for Ludlow's suitcase — which he never had, by the way. We were eventually taken over to the camp and to our respective huts, and I was introduced to my comfortable bed. It was the first palliasse I'd ever seen in my life. I thought, How in the heck am I going to sleep there? In a hut with 20 other chappies. It was quite an experience for me.

The next morning, first of all we had the sergeant-major come round right on the tick of six o'clock, and see that everybody was up and about. Then we had a commanding officer give us our instructions for the day. We spent most of the first morning at the quartermaster's store getting our outfits. I was given a pair of denims that would have fitted a seven-foot bloke. I'm only five foot five.

When I had to sign the papers for my previous job, I put 'Findlay's Bakery'. I didn't say that I was just a driver. They naturally thought, Well, here's a boy we want in the cookhouse. When they found out what a good cook I was, I don't know why, to this day, but I didn't last in the cookhouse more than a couple of hours.

Can you remember hearing that war had been declared?
Yes. In Hastings a group of us used to get around together, and we were all at a party one night. A phone call came through that war had been declared. The party went on, but in a very gloomy sort of a way. Everybody was knocked flat. It all went quiet, and half an hour later there was no party and everybody went home. It was the last thing in the world I thought would happen.

I belonged to the West End tennis club in Hastings. In that club there was a chap called Mick Thompson, and my best friend, Ray Vestey. The three of us joined up together and we finished up in the same hut at Trentham, which was quite good. I was sorry when I got transferred over to camp staff. I had to leave them, which didn't make me happy at the time.

They went overseas?
Yes. Mick returned home, but unfortunately Ray was killed over there.

Harry went into camp with the Hawke's Bay second training unit in June 1940 and was to have gone overseas with the Fourth Echelon.

One night I was put on guard duty and I struck the main gates for the camp. I went on around about nine o'clock at night and I was there till six o'clock the next morning. I'm quite sure every officer in the camp had leave that night, because I seemed to be doing nothing else but 'Shoulder arms! Shoulder

Above: *From left: Harry Spencer, Ray Vestey and Mick Thompson at Trentham.* Harry Spencer collection
Right: *Harry Spencer slopes arms.* Harry Spencer collection

arms!' By the end of the night I could hardly lift my rifle. I'm only a little fella and they're heavy rifles. You used to have to shoulder arms as these officers came in, and salute them. I reported to the RAP that morning and they told me that I had flat feet and weak eyes. They transferred me to camp staff. They said that I wouldn't be able to stand up to the sand in the desert, and things like that. Whether that was right or not, I had to take their word for it.

Can you remember how you felt that day?
Most disappointed, because my two close friends were on their way over, and I was left out. I felt that it was my fault, but it wasn't really.

When you enlisted, had they given you a medical test then?
Yes. We went to the Hastings drill hall. We were given a proper test. There was a doctor and a lot of Army personnel. I passed the test all right. Everything was all right.

I honestly would have liked to have gone overseas, not that I wanted to be a hero or anything like that, but I thought, All my cobbers are going. Why should I be left behind?

Despite the disappointment of not going overseas, Harry enjoyed army life at Trentham.

The hut was good. There were 20 beds in the hut, with straw palliasses. The first night the straw was sticking through into my bottom, but after about three nights it was lovely to get into it. You soon got used to it, and if you were tired enough you'd sleep anywhere. I can't remember my palliasse ever being replaced, so it was quite flat in the finish. They were building huts. At Trentham, I can't remember any tents. We were all billeted in huts, the whole lot of us, even the officers. They had little units to themselves, very similar to a little motel.

How did they wake you up?
They always played reveille every morning, and you were given about 10 minutes. Then our sergeant-

major would come in and you'd hear a big yell from the door, 'Feet on the floor!' Then he would turn around and march off, and, just as he got to the door, he'd bellow, 'I'll be back!'

When you got up in the morning, the first thing you did was make your bed. At around 10 o'clock there'd be an officer and a sergeant (what we called the 'officer of the day') come around and inspect every hut, every bed. If you weren't tidy, he'd untidy it for you and let you know that he wasn't happy with it. They were very strict on that. Everyone had a little locker beside his bed, and your dress uniform would be always left there, but you practically lived in your denims. You'd have to get into uniform at night time for your evening meal.

When you weren't drilling, you were sitting on the side of your bed polishing your brassware. That used to be a heck of a job, because once you were on parade the officer would have a strict look at all your brassware — buttons and badges — and if it wasn't polished up, you knew about it.

We had church parade every Sunday morning, and you had to have a very good reason if you weren't to attend church parade. Each denomination had their own parade.

Tell me about the training you had when you first got there.
When I first went into camp, we were taken to our respective huts. The next morning, after the quartermaster, we more or less had a free day. The second day we started our drill. I loved that part of it. We used to go marching. Every second afternoon we'd march out of camp on a route march.

Later on we'd have charging practice. You'd have a dummy and your army rifle with your bayonet on the end of it, and you'd charge and see how you got on with the dummy. We had a lot of that. Also, we had a reasonably high fence put in front of us and it was your job to get over the other side of it. If you were a bit on the slow side, the officer used to let you know about it.

Tell me about your shooting practice.
I was terribly nervous marching down to the rifle range, which was just outside the Trentham camp. There was quite a big hill behind the targets. We were given our targets and we had to lie on the ground. There'd only be six feet between each soldier lying there, and we all had our own target, and then we were told to fire. The noise of the firing from both sides of you — there was no such thing as having ear muffs or anything at all like that, you just had to take it. Poor old me, I just shut my eyes and pulled the trigger, and I don't think I was even hitting the hill behind the target, let alone

the target. I well remember that first day. I didn't know how to hold a rifle. The instructor was telling me what to do, told me it would kick back, but I had no idea it was going to kick back that hard. I couldn't touch my shoulder that night, it was that sore. But after about three or four days I never noticed it. It was just the way you held your rifle. If you held your rifle properly it didn't buck.

After three or four days down there, I got to like it and, strange as it may seem, I became quite a good shot. Sometimes I'd ask if there was extra practice on the rifle range just to get down there. I thoroughly enjoyed it. After about a month or six weeks of that, I was transferred to the Bren gun unit, where I was put as an instructor.

Trentham camp and racecourse. ATL, S.C. Smith Collection, G-47866-1/2

Following his transfer to camp staff, Harry went into the supply and transport unit at Trentham, where he ended up working in the stores.

Before I went into the stores, my first job was with two other chappies, Archie Fox and Bill McMaster. I was put on a coal truck with them. Our job was to see that the four main cookhouses and the showers had coal and coke for their firing and heating. Every afternoon we had to go down to the coal and coke yards in Petone, get our load, then come back and deliver it round to the different cookhouses. It was pretty hard work, but we used to have our spare moments. When we got down to Petone, practically every afternoon we'd go into the working men's club and get as much beer into us as we possibly could, as quick as we could. One time we didn't get back to the camp till five o'clock in the afternoon, and by the time we'd finished delivering it, it was seven o'clock. All our cobbers said it was a shame that these three fellas had got such long hours. Little did they know where we'd been all the afternoon.

I remember a chap, Alf Jenkins, who had a gymnasium in Wellington. He was a very keen soccer enthusiast and also a very keen softball enthusiast. I'd never played soccer in my life before, but one afternoon he asked me to have a game of soccer, ordered me to play. I forgot all about the coal — we all did — so we didn't go down to Petone that afternoon for the coal and coke until about five o'clock, and then it was a mile too late. People were worrying about the poor officers. They came up to me and said, 'We had to have a shower in cold water this morning.' I said, 'What a shame. What a shame.' Little did they know that I was one of the ones responsible for it.

What were your shower blocks like?
We didn't have a shower to ourselves. As soon as one got empty you'd hop in for your shot. There was no privacy. I didn't like it at all. I'd never been in anything like that before in my life and I was rather bashful, but it didn't take me long to learn to get over that. If you didn't, you were gone a million. We had a shower every morning. There was always hot water. When I had a shower, I always saw that there was plenty of hot water.

I well remember getting my first stripe to make me a lance corporal. The first day I walked round, looking at my arm all day long. I didn't know whether I was Governor-General or who I was. I quickly rose through the ranks and got to sergeant, then to staff sergeant. Once I got into the sergeants' mess we had proper knives and forks, and you were waited on and all that. It was a different world altogether.

I was chief storeman out in the stores. The boys in the office would allocate a quota for each cookhouse, and it was my job, when they gave me the allocations, to get each one ready and send it off to each cookhouse, each morning. That was a most interesting job, because some days you'd have too much of something and not enough of the other, and have to work everything out. You had to see each cookhouse had its rations for the day.

How many cookhouses were there?
There was first training unit, second and third training units, and Army School.

What about when the WAACs arrived? Were there any changes then to the way you did things?
In the supply and transport we had two WAACs, and they did a fantastic job. They worked well with the men, but there was no such thing as getting friendly with them or anything at all like that. That would be taboo. They had their own units and they lived well away from the boys.

Particularly at Trentham, there were plenty of officers and one did lots and lots of saluting. You had to bring your arm up a certain way. We did have officers who were fairly easy-going, but we also had those who, if you didn't salute properly, would pull you up and tell you. I had a very close friend [who was an officer]. We used to go on leave into Wellington, we were very close cobbers. We'd go to the troop train to go back to camp after being on leave for the weekend, and he would go into his carriage amongst all the officers, I'd have to go amongst the troops. Before I left, I used to stand there and salute him. I didn't like that very much, but it had to be done.

We only got the weekend once a fortnight, but if you misbehaved in any way at all your leave would be cancelled.

Harry would spend his weekend leave with his wife, Sylvia Lewis, whom he had married in Hastings in 1941 after learning that he was not to be posted overseas. After

Harry and his wife, Sylvia. Harry Spencer collection

their marriage, Sylvia came to live in Wellington, where she worked for the YMCA. She became
pregnant, but the baby died soon after birth. The couple's twin boys, Ken and John, were born
in 1944. The twins spent the first months of their life at the Karitane Hospital in Melrose.
Harry got compassionate leave every night during this time.

As well as weekend leave, the soldiers at Trentham could attend concerts in the Army School
hall on Tuesday nights. The concerts were run by Mrs Dennistoun-Wood.

She was very well known for going around and entertaining the troops wherever she possibly could. Henry Rudolph and his singers — he called them The Melody Maids — were well known around the Wellington area, and they used to come in and put on a lovely show for us. The old hall would be packed. We had some singers from the camp. It was surprising, some of the really class singers that were there. They used to be very good.

What songs would they sing?
Just what they'd sing outside camp. Proper classical songs and all sorts of stuff. There was always the hard case who'd sing 'Goodnight Sergeant-Major', or something like that.

Were they slightly risqué, those songs?
Oh yes, yes, yes. Very much so.

And was Mrs Dennistoun-Wood still there then?
Oh yes. She was a great sport.

A bit later on, we formed a softball team. We had a couple of good softballers. There was one chappie, Ron McLaughlin, who was a very, very good softball player. His family were all players and took part in forming the softball association in Wellington.

Of a Saturday morning, we'd pick a team from those who were on leave — you could only pick the players who were on leave. A man from Denhard's Bakery would come out and deliver the bread about eleven o'clock of a Saturday morning, and on his way out, he would be going through the gates with eleven softballers inside the van. We used to go to the Occidental Hotel; that was our first port of call. We'd all hop out there and go in for a few beers. Our softball game started at two o'clock in the afternoon. We'd leave the Occidental about half past one, all in very good moods. We had a chap,

Harry (front row, centre) with his softball team. Harry Spencer collection

Bill McMaster, who had bad eyesight. He was running from one base to the other and didn't see the chappie standing on the base, who was only a little light fellow. Bill bowled him about ten yards when he got to his base and hit him.

The Army Education Welfare Service — did you have anything to do with that?
Yes. We were invited to go along to different schools of a night time. This was happening quite a lot when the war was coming to an end. Plastics were just coming onto the market. A bloke said to me one day, 'Harry, if I were you, I'd go and learn all you possibly can about plastics. There'll be plenty of work and plastics is the coming thing.' I'd never heard of it before and I decided it was not for me. I've been sorry ever since that I didn't take it on, because today everything is plastic. They gave you the opportunity to learn practically any career that you wanted to take on. There was someone to help you along with it. You had to do it in your own time, of course, but it was a big thing, and, as it went on, it got bigger and bigger. It was sort of a rehabilitation thing. It was getting you used to being back in the ordinary way of life again.

Left: *Construction of stores in the Hutt Valley for use by US troops.* ATL, John Pascoe Collection, F-365-1/4
Opposite: *Johnsonville, 1946.* ATL, Evening Post Collection, PAColl-8557-42

Did you think the Japanese might invade New Zealand?

We were waiting for it every day. Just waiting for it every day. People like myself who didn't know would say, What the heck is going to stop them? Thank goodness that they didn't get down this far.

When the Americans came to town, I had one experience. I'm only five foot five, so I'm pretty short. One night I was on leave and half a dozen of us went down to a hotel at Taita and were having a pretty merry time. I got myself into a bit of trouble and one chap started to have me on, wanted to fight me. Anyway, there was a Yank and his nickname was Happy. He came up there and took my part for no reason at all. He could have got into all sorts of trouble. He stopped me from getting a hiding, anyway, and I had a lot of admiration for them after that.

Did it ever occur to you that the Allies might not win the war?

You always had that in your mind, but your main thoughts were, How long is this going to go on for? How long am I going to be here? What's going to happen after it's over? What will happen to us? I was pleased when the end did come. I can remember jumping up and down and cheering, going to Courtenay Place that night.

> *Harry was based at Trentham camp for four and a half years, and was discharged in March 1945, before the war ended. After the war, he worked in a friend's battery factory in Wellington for 17 years, ending up as marketing manager. He then set up his own battery factory in Petone, and after about eight years sold it to another firm, although he kept working there until he retired.*

Did you find it hard being a civilian again?

I found the life completely different. I missed the Army life. Some of them used to call me 'Wombat' because I originally came from Australia, and I suppose they called me other names, but I didn't hear

them. In there, I was one of the boys, and when I came out into a civvy life it was completely different. It took me such a long time to adapt to being told by one of my fellow workmates what to do, and things like that.

Harry and Sylvia lived with their twin boys in the Wellington suburb of Khandallah.

Our place had just the one bedroom, and the bed nearly filled the room. By the time we got a cot in with the twins, that properly filled it. My poor wife, she used to have to do the washing in the bath. There was no wash-house. They were pretty hard times. There wasn't a lot of money around. By the time I'd paid 35 shillings a week rent, there wasn't a lot left for the rest of us.

It took me a long time to put up with my family. I was used to a big crowd of men around me all the time, and then to come home to a quiet house with the family . . . I was very easily upset. Thank goodness, I didn't stay like that very long — perhaps six months. After that I settled down. I had my gratuity, which came to the total value of £50, and I borrowed some money off a chap who was in camp with me and I bought a section. When I bought that, the repatriation board lent me £1500 and I was able to put a house on the section for that. That was one of the best things I ever did after the war.

Harry's house was in Johnsonville, where he still lives. His wife died in 1994.

I look forward to Anzac Day because we always have a good speaker and it brings a lot of old memories back to me. I do appreciate it. I enjoy it. I think of friends. I miss old Ray.

'I COULDN'T KILL'

Mervyn BROWNE,
Conscientious objector

Merv was born in Wanganui in 1922, the son of Martha and Theodore Browne. He attended Gonville School and Wanganui Technical College before beginning a printer's apprenticeship at the **Wanganui Herald**. *Merv and his parents were active members of the Methodist Church, which took, in the inter-war years, a strongly pacifist stance under such ministers as Ormond Burton, and, in Wanganui, the Reverend 'Tubby' Martin.*

Were you aware that it was likely there was going to be another war?

Yes. I can remember clearly coming out of the pictures. There'd been a flash on the screen to say Germany had invaded Poland, and I looked up to the sky, quite expecting there to be bombers coming over. I thought it was going to be like that. Of course it wasn't.

In August 1941, Merv's name was drawn in the 18-year-olds' military ballot.

I went to the medical examination — I didn't care about that. By that time I had a strong belief that I couldn't kill. It was a personal thing. At that stage I didn't belong to any peace organisation except the church. I was only a very late and insignificant member of the Christian Pacifist Society, which was quite strong in Wanganui.

Did that happen suddenly or over a period of time?

I think it was growing. Mum and Dad were both giving me the same message. Dad often spoke about his feelings — the disappointment that the First World War hadn't achieved what he'd hoped it would. Later in the war, he publicly resigned from the RSA in protest at their harsh attitude to conchies.

Previous page: *Red Compound, Hautu detention camp, 1943.* ATL, A.C. Barrington Collection, F-37725-1/2
Above: *Merv Browne, Hautu detention camp, 1943.* Mervyn Browne collection

Above: *Wellington's* Evening Post *reports the outbreak of the Second World War.* ATL, War History Collection, F-66962-1/2
Inset: *Wanganui, 1925.* ATL, S.C. Smith Collection, G-45550-1/2

Merv's decision to refuse military service affected his relations with his workmates at the **Wanganui Herald.**

There must have been a majority of them who felt that I shouldn't be allowed to continue working with them, so they took a petition to the management asking that I be dismissed. The management weren't prepared to do that, so I carried on working. They were somewhat difficult days, but we got through — partly because I was very active in sports and so I met up with them in other ways, on the rugby field or at athletics.

People who previously had not made their ideas known were quite prepared to say, 'We're all for this war', and they felt that I was a leper. The feeling of rejection was very strong, but I'd decided that this was me. It had got nothing to do with anybody else, and I feel that in no way was I ever proselytising about it. I wasn't very public, even, about it.

Under the National Service Emergency Regulations of 1940, Merv could have appealed against his military service to the Armed Forces Appeal Board on grounds of conscience. He decided not to after his close friend Jack had his appeal turned down, because he felt that the board was biased against conscientious objectors.

I thought, I can't imagine anyone more sincere than Jack. I'm not going to go through with it, so I notified them that I wouldn't be applying for a dispensation.

In September 1941, he received a summons to appear at Wanganui Court because he had failed to report for military duties.

That was an ordeal for an 18-year-old. You normally went to court because you'd done something wrong, and I didn't feel I'd done anything wrong. It was all very formal, but very brief, and I was dismissed and given one month's hard labour. It was to be expected, but it was hard when the door was slammed shut. The prison in Wanganui is right in the middle of town, and I could scramble up on my canvas hammock in the cell and look out the bars and see my mates going to work. I was in the cell for 16 hours of the day, and for 8 hours you were either being searched or being led around or doing some gardening. They had a big vegetable garden there. The 16 hours were a long, long time. I remember I bought myself a chess set before I went to prison, only I couldn't find anyone in the prison who played chess. You had times in the weekend where you were sitting around together in an open enclosure, mainly playing cards.

When you went to court, did you have support?
My parents were there and also the Methodist minister. He wasn't going to be put down. He had a say.

What about your friends? How did they react?

It's interesting — the only friends who came to visit me in prison were some adults from the church. People I respected. I think you only had an hour, once a week. It was only for a month.

What happened at the end of the month?

When they released me, the Army was waiting for me at the gates. It was all by arrangement. The government hadn't planned [on how to deal with objectors], so we were sent to Waiouru military barracks. They didn't want us. By that time [conscientious objectors] were coming from all round the district. I think there'd have been about a dozen or more of us.

Being at Waiouru was a very interesting experience, because there were troops preparing to go overseas. On one occasion we had 'Brushy' Mitchell, a former All Black, come and talk with us quite seriously about why we were not going to the war. He was quite genuinely interested, not condemnatory. He acknowledged people could be different.

It was quite an experience for us, because we were a disparate group. We had Jehovah's Witnesses and a Communist, some of us from the church background. I remember the group was particularly stimulated by Jimmy Warburton and Bob Durrant. These two were thinkers, philosophers. Both of them held university posts later. So it gave those of us who hadn't had that opportunity the time to think about the philosophy of what was involved. It was good. Bob would be taken up under guard to see the camp commandant. They didn't know that Bob and Colonel Powles were talking philosophy.

We only got out for an exercise period, usually about an hour, but for the rest of the day we were confined to the barrack. There were separate cells, but there was a room where we could eat and sit around together. Good Army food, good basic stuff.

Did everybody take part in those talks about the reasons they were there?

Pretty well, yes. Some of the extreme religios weren't so keen because their case was already cut and dried. There was no moving from it.

How did you get on with them?

Very well. The biggest group was Assemblies of God. They were people with very strong commitments, and they were the same groups that were being put into concentration camps in Germany — mainly

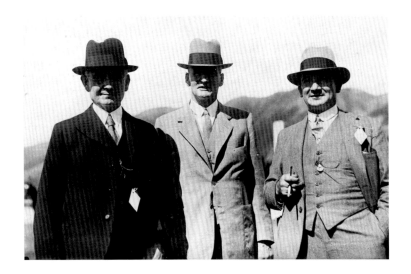

*From left: Labour politicians
Michael Joseph Savage,
Mark Fagan and Paddy Webb.*
ATL, PAColl-8845

Jehovah's Witnesses, but other groups also — because they were pacifist.

Were you offered the option of doing non-combatant work?
I think that if I'd gone a bit further along the military line I would have been, but I already knew that a good mate of mine went into the Army prepared to take non-combatant service. He was given an assurance that he would do ambulance work and medical work, but even before I went into prison I saw a photograph of him with a rifle slung over his shoulder. He couldn't get out at that stage, he was trapped. So it really wasn't an option at all for me.

> *After a month at Waiouru, the group was sent to Mt Eden Prison for two weeks because the authorities had not organised anywhere else for them to go. In November 1941, after a week in police cells in Hamilton, where they were sentenced to defaulters' detention for the duration of the war, the group arrived at Strathmore detention camp, near Reporoa.*

It was a place of, almost, healing. I got to know people a bit better. We were in Public Works camp tents. I had some very interesting tent mates. Allan Nixon, who was later assistant professor of law at Auckland, and a chap called Jack Crichton, who was a very highly regarded commercial law solicitor — a person a lot older than most of us. He would have been nearly 50. A very fine person. There was a bit more opportunity to talk with people.

They'd put up 10-foot-high barbed wire fences around the camp area. It was a scrubby area with pine trees out to Kaingaroa Forest — which had been planted by Paddy Webb and other MPs who were now in the government and running the war, but who'd been imprisoned in the First World War for opposing conscription.

Did you have a uniform?

Not really. They gave us a pair of moleskin trousers and a grey shirt. I don't know whether they'd designed it themselves, I don't think so. They must have just had it there. We were given a welcome by the camp commandant, who was a chap by the name of Duffy, and the intention was for us to do useful work for society. That's how it started off. We entered into this with a fair bit of enthusiasm, breaking in the land for returning soldiers, perhaps, and that's what it became. Grubbing scrub that grew up about as fast behind us as it grew in front of us. It was a bit depressing. We had to build a sheep dip

Merv Browne (back) at Hautu detention camp, 1943. ATL, A.C. Barrington Collection, F-37724-1/2

on one occasion, and that was a useful exercise. They were trying at that stage to isolate us and have us do some useful work.

That camp became by far the biggest camp. I think it would possibly have held 250 or more.

There were men at Strathmore from a wide range of backgrounds.

I can think of two jockeys, for instance, and you don't think of jockeys being conscientious objectors to war. Practically everybody was almost bristling with a conviction. They saw no rhyme nor reason in killing people in order to get a political decision. Something other than two peoples standing opposite one another and just kill, kill, kill, kill, kill. They're not the people who are going to make the decisions. It's somebody else who's going to make a decision as to whether the war should continue or end. As we so frequently said, 'Men have decided that this is the way; well, men can do some more thinking and decide for another way.'

My father and younger brother biked all the way from Wanganui to visit me. It was good to see them.

Merv was at Strathmore until March 1942, when he was transferred to Hautu detention camp, near Turangi.

It wasn't till March 1944 that I refused work. I was at Hautu all that time, and in that time the camp had changed dramatically. A hospital unit had been built. We had a matron and a nurse there. The *Maui Pomare*, the boat that used to

Detention camp, showing conscientious objectors, huts and barbed-wire fence.
ATL, Nightingall/Morrell Collection,
PAColl-7167-04-05-2

trade around the Pacific, was taken out of service and her turbines were set up so Hautu had its own power house. Then the fences were doubled and I think heightened, so that the screws — as we called them, the warders — could walk around between the wire fences and keep an eye, day and night. Later they put floodlights up too. We felt very strongly that it was becoming [like a POW camp] — I don't know whether it happened like that in Germany, but it was the progression of things. The isolation of the camp meant it was very difficult to get to. The type of supervision we had by the guards was pathetic really. They were almost unemployable.

> *Merv had met his close friend, Chris Palmer, at Hautu. In March 1944, Merv, along with some of the other men at Hautu, decided that they would refuse to work.*

What made you decide that?

Well, in our discussions in the gangs, as we worked, it was a pretty general contention that the camps had radically changed, so we refused work. We were transferred back to Strathmore, and from there Chris and I escaped in 1944, on May 14th.

Some others did different things. A couple of wharfies decided that they would escape and go back to Auckland. They got caught before they got there. It seems so ludicrous, looking back on it now, that two youths would be able to say it was time a negotiated peace took place as everything seemed to be ripe for it — [particularly given] the state of the Germans after they'd been into Russia. It seemed to us it lent itself to a negotiated peace, so we arranged with friends to get some pamphlets down to Wellington, and then we published one other down there. We just bided our time until we thought we could safely escape from Strathmore.

It really was very tense, but we were quite relaxed about it, strangely enough. We had to crawl under two barbed-wire fences and then cross perhaps half a mile of fairly flat, exposed, scrubby country. A chap had asked could he come out with us. He wanted to get back to his mother in Christchurch, who was very elderly. He was in his forties and he needed to give her some support. We said, 'OK, Len, you can come with us, but we're going to separate. As soon as we get through the fences and out into the scrub, we'll separate.' We were younger and could travel much faster, for one thing.

Len, stupidly, didn't follow our pattern — you lay on your back, and you pushed the wire out of the way. You could see what you were doing. He went out on his stomach and got his jersey caught.

We were waiting for the guards to come around. It was hair-raising. We left him as soon as we were out of the grounds, and went up into the Kaingaroa Forest. We knew we were going south-south-east to get onto the Taupo–Napier road.

Any particular reason for heading to Napier?
Yes. We wanted to go to Wellington, and we thought it was better to go via Napier than to try and go out to National Park and get on the train. We only walked at night, and then we slept or just kept out of the way during the daytime somewhere off the side of the road. It took us about four or five days, I think, to get to Napier, and there we met up with a former guard from Hautu who'd been manpowered into his job but didn't like it, so he'd gone back to the freezing works where he'd been working previously. He'd come to me: 'I might be able to help you.' He lent us a bike, a real boneshaker. Chris's legs were too long if he sat on the bar and I tried to double him, so instead we used a system where one of us biked about 10 power poles then left the bike for the other one who was walking behind, and then the person who'd been riding walked on. This worked until I missed the bike. Neither of us knew that the bike was still way back. I went back and got it, and shortly after that we got rid of the bike because the pedal crank broke. We kept walking towards Woodville. We'd arranged to have some clothes sent there, some civvy clothes, by Chris's parents. We went to the Methodist minister — to find there was no one at home. We were getting a bit anxious, but we finally found a note saying that the clothes were in the wash-house, so we got changed and went on to Wellington separately, by train.

How did you organise to get the clothes in Woodville?
We used to write on cigarette papers and pass these notes to willing visitors. So tiny. Just brief details of what we were doing, or what we needed. There were lots of Aucklanders visiting Strathmore.

What about food?
We had a tin of milk powder and cocoa with some sugar, all mixed up together, and we largely existed on drinks. We thought that would give us a bit of stamina, so we had a tin of this stuff. I think we might have had a few vegies once or twice. We had to go through a camp in the Kaingaroa Forest. The dogs barked and we were sure that somebody was going to come and grab us, but we got through and were just getting out of the camp when we saw great stacks of potatoes. We thought, They won't miss one

or two potatoes. We'll have potatoes tomorrow. Which we did.

We had a semi-civilian kit which had been made by a mate who worked in the machine shop and had a sewing machine. They repaired people's clothes and that sort of thing at the camp. Chris had a real kinship with him because they were both beekeepers. We had shorts and a heavy cloth shirt, which made us look a bit like civilians.

The others at Strathmore, they were happy to support you?

Some were, and some were strongly opposed to us, because inevitably we knew that it would aggravate conditions within the camp. The more people escape, every time the screw goes down a bit further, and we had to accept this. We sometimes felt a little bit guilty about it, but not too guilty.

Minister of Defence Fred Jones with his son. ATL, New Zealand Free Lance Collection, PAColl-8602-39

We were caught out the night before we left because we were dyeing these clothes — I don't know where we got the dye from, somebody must have brought it in. What had happened was that they found our clothes drying in an empty hut. One of the warders had gone in for a sleep, probably, and found these clothes. They had a show of hands after the midday meal because this dye would show on somebody's hands, and as I came up to the table the warder said, 'Oh Browne, get going. You're not likely to be stupid enough to do this sort of thing.'

When we got to Wellington I stayed with the Carmans, a tremendous couple, and their five kids out at Tawa. Chris was in town somewhere. We met up and we distributed the pamphlets. I distributed pamphlets also for Arthur Carman, who was standing for the county council.

We agreed that we weren't going to stay out more than a month. We both went up to Parliament, and didn't see the minister, Fred Jones. We were told to come again. I said, 'I'll go down to Pigeon Park in Courtenay Place.' I'd never spoken publicly before. There were some soldiers who were a bit under the weather. It was Friday night and they were celebrating, and making things a bit noisy and difficult. The police came in and arrested me. That was good — I'd run out of things to say.

Open-air meetings where pacifists spoke against the conflict had been held in Wellington's Pigeon Park throughout the war. Such meetings became much more sporadic as the war continued, however, as many of the speakers were imprisoned or sent to the detention camps and so were effectively removed from the public arena.

The same day, Chris had been arrested. He'd gone back to Parliament and was told, 'Get moving. All the Minister can do is ring the bell here and the police will come and pick you up.' So they did that. That's what we wanted.

While we were there, my mother came down to see me. She was staying with a friend of hers, Blanche Clemenceau, who was housekeeper at the French Legation. Mum and Blanche were walking along a fairly empty Lambton Quay, in the evening, where we'd arranged to meet, and suddenly, who should I see coming along but a policeman, doing the beat. I didn't know what to say, but I greeted Mum and Blanche and we tried to look as normal as possible. He didn't know who I was, fortunately. It was really good. We found a quiet place to talk, and then they had to be on their way.

In June 1944, Merv and Chris Palmer were sentenced to three months' hard labour for escaping from Strathmore detention camp. They spent one month at Mt Crawford in Wellington and two months at Wi Tako (now Rimutaka) Prison in Upper Hutt. In September 1944, Merv and Chris were sent to Hautu detention camp, where they again refused to work. They were put in solitary confinement.

We were put in what they called the Red Compound, a punishment compound. That was pretty harsh. We had a tiny hut, with inadequate bedding which was removed each morning. The temperatures were often as low as 10-degree frosts. You were all day sitting in a hut, except for an hour's exercise. Twenty-three hours a day in that little hut. It was a bit restricting. I think they gave us a Bible and one other book. I was reading about native birds and trying to remember the names of them. Chris was in another hut. I didn't see anything of him, but he was there somewhere. We had restricted rations, some of the time very restricted.

A conscientious objector in the doorway of his hut.
ATL, Nightingall/Morrell Collection, PAColl-7167-04-19-1

You mean bread and water?
Not quite.

On 12 December 1944, I was taken to Rotorua Court and from there sentenced to imprisonment, as distinct from detention camp. Detention camp didn't want to see me again. I was imprisoned for the duration of the war. This is significant, because the friend I mentioned earlier, Jack Crichton, the solicitor, maintained that he was sentenced for the duration of the war. At that time the war was with Germany and then later it was Japan, so he maintained that when the war with Germany was completed, he should be free. He pleaded his case in court and Mr Justice Fair in Hamilton agreed with his contention.

There's no other situation where a person has an indefinite sentence. If a person is, say, imprisoned for psychiatric reasons, there's always a proviso about re-examination, but for us it was just until they chose to release us. I wasn't released until 1946, on 23 May. The war was long, long over.

What was it like in that tiny little room? How did you deal with that mentally?
I don't know, I can't remember. The days dragged on.

What was the reason you were sent from the Red Compound at Hautu to prison?
I think they were getting a bit worried about us, health-wise. I *think* so. It was cold, freezing. I went to Waikune — no longer a prison — just south of National Park. It was a dump. The only difference about this camp was that it had a superintendent who was quite exceptional. His name was Jeremiah Quill. He had a son in the priesthood, and a wife who was very compassionate. They weren't young, either of them. I remember one occasion, Christmas came around and Jeremiah had one of our blokes on bread and water. Mrs Quill came to the exercise yard, and here were all these bodies out in the pumice exercise yard. Filthy thing, with the huts all around it, facing in towards it. She called out, 'Jeremiah!' 'Yes, my

dear.' 'Jeremiah, I understand you have a man on bread and water, and it's Christmas today. There'll be no Christmas dinner for you until he is released.' In front of everyone! Jeremiah said, 'Right, my dear.' He was a character, he really was.

> *Merv met his fiancée, Marjorie Clark, through her cousin, Noel Ginn, who was in Hautu Camp. The couple carried on their courtship by correspondence and became engaged while Merv was still at Hautu.*

Marj biked up to see me at Waikune from Wanganui. She didn't know what to expect, but Quill said when she went in to ask for permission, 'Right, you may have all day.' Now what on earth do you do, all day, two of you sitting six feet away from one another? You're meant to express your feelings and your thoughts for the future and all sorts of things. It was hopeless. Of course, there was a screw all the time in the corner.

> *Chris Palmer had been sent to Rangipo Prison. Merv thinks there were around seven conscientious objectors at Waikune. They did road maintenance, then later were transferred to Makatote quarry.*

We were cracking big rocks into little rocks into smaller rocks until they were small enough to put in the crusher. It was an utter waste of labour. All along, wherever we got to, every time we went before the judge or magistrate, we made the same plea: 'Look, we'll do anything useful, anything at all.' We offered to work in hospitals, we offered help at the time of the Masterton earthquake, various needs we could have met with our particular skills. No. They just wanted to keep us out of sight, and also to punish us. That was an interesting extra dimension.

We decided this was ridiculous. We were going to get into the public eye somehow and say other things.

Was there agitation outside?

Yes, it was going on all the time. People like Arthur Carman or Ron Howell in Auckland, and many people who were very good at putting a pamphlet out on the old Gestetner.

Did you know that was going on?

Yes, we did. It heartened us.

We decided that we were going to refuse work. On 12 February, we refused work, about six of us. Justices of the peace, two of them, came, and they constituted a magistrate. We were sentenced to solitary confinement, which was ridiculous — we were already in solitary confinement — and threatened with 30 days in chains. Utterly ridiculous, but it was in the book of rules. Later, when I was at Mt Eden, I saw the rings — they had them up on the wall — where they used to actually chain prisoners, with their feet barely on the ground. They were taken down for an hour at midnight. Incredible. So we were threatened with this, and we laughed like anything about it afterwards. It sounded very grim at the time.

That was in February, and in March we were taken to Auckland because we'd started a hunger strike. There were only three of us left on it. Others had had to give in for various reasons. We were determined; we'd discussed it. We weren't going to kill ourselves, but we were going to take it for a long time. At Waikune we were still under solitary confinement, this alleged solitary confinement. It was quite ridiculous, because the compound was such that they couldn't stop us having conversations. We used to have dictionary quizzes, and those who studied Latin won every time. Nevertheless, it was a pretty restricted time. We started the hunger strike, and it was Ian Hamilton, Bruce McAlpine and myself who were finally transferred to Auckland because we'd gone on a bit long.

The three men were transferred to Mt Eden Prison on 16 April 1945.

We continued to strike there. That was probably the grimmest time that I had. We were put down in the . . . well, I call it the dungeons. It was the cells below the prison itself. The worst part was exercise time — you had an hour's exercise — which was in the hanging yard. You went into a tiny yard with great walls,

Supporters of conscientious objectors preparing a publication.
ATL, Nightingall/Morrell Collection, PAColl-7167-04-49-1

about twenty feet high, all around you. Higher than that on the prison side. You could hear the kids' voices from the grammar school, and there was the concrete bath where they laid the body after the hanging. It really was quite grim.

Later, I didn't try to go out into the yard because I needed something to hang on to. I did 36 days without food. Every day they'd bring the midday meal and put it on the table in front of me and come back and always check to see that I hadn't had any. At no time did they get the doctor to examine me. I had water only, for 36 days.

Were you ever tempted?

No, no. You get to the stage where you're not even interested. Bruce and Ian sent me messages to say, 'C'mon, enough's enough, Merv.' I didn't see them, but messages came by various means. Sometimes as they were going out to exercise the warder would be up opening the next door, and they'd have a yarn through the door. I said, 'I'll be OK. Just give me a day or two. I'll decide.' But meanwhile the message was going out. Marj was writing to the Minister saying that the war had been over so long now, and I still had no remission.

What happened in the end that made you decide to stop?

I decided it was enough. They took me up to the so-called hospital room, and fed me semolina. I'd never had it before.

Merv was not given a medical examination after his hunger strike.

I was discharged from Mt Eden on 23 May 1946, with a rail ticket to Wanganui and an account for £19 for prison infringements — refusal to attend designated church services, protesting at injustices to other prisoners, and such things. I didn't even have enough for a cup of tea or a phone call. They just opened the door and I had to struggle up Khyber Pass with a suitcase full of books and things. I was pretty sick then, too.

Marj was at Marton to meet me. It really was fantastic. The message had got through somehow.

Could you believe you were out?
No, it was a bit unreal.

Merv had contracted tuberculosis while in detention. He thinks that probably happened at Waikune, where many of the men had the disease and the prisoners had to share all the facilities. It took him many years to recover. He and Marjorie married in 1946 and have two daughters and two sons. The couple went to Riverside Community, near Nelson, in 1949, and currently live in Hamilton.

The extract on the right is taken from one of the pamphlets produced by Merv Browne and Chris Palmer.

WE FULLY APPRECIATE THE COURAGE AND SELF-SACRIFICE OF THE MEN AND WOMEN IN THE ARMED FORCES.
The stand we have taken is in no way critical of these people, but it is an emphatic protest against a system which breeds war, a system which demands as the price of its existence that millions of young lives must be destroyed by the beastliness of war, instead of being permitted to develop to the full in some peaceful, creative work.

WE URGE . . . PEACE NOW BY NEGOTIATION.
Sooner or later the peoples of the world will have to get together to discuss peace terms. **Why not now?** Stop and think what every day of war means in terms of human life, in suffering and tragedy, in the collapse of morality, and the prostitution of ideals and principles. **Wars are man-made and can therefore be stopped when men decide to stop them.**

'I CHOSE
TO BE A PILOT'

George JUDGE, 437465, Flight Sergeant, RNZAF

George Judge served in the Home Guard, the Army and the Air Force during the war. He was born in Wanganui in July 1923. His father Edwin was a linesman, and his mother Christina had emigrated to New Zealand from Scotland after the First World War. The Judge family moved to Ohakune and then Gisborne, where George attended school. He began work as a cadet in the Maori Affairs Department in Gisborne in 1940.

Can you remember hearing that the war had been declared?

I was at high school. Oh yes, we knew all about it. The papers were pretty full of the crisis. Chamberlain, and things building up, the invasion of Czechoslovakia and Poland, but we were so far away that it didn't come too close for us in New Zealand.

I worked voluntarily for the local Territorial headquarters for a while, where they sent out notices for those they were calling up. As soon as they formed the Home Guard, I was keen to get into it. A few young fellas, and one or two older First War men were in charge.

What sorts of things did you do in the Home Guard?

Very little, really. We got together, did a bit of marching and watch-keeping on Kaiti Hill in Gisborne. They maintained some sort of a guard. You could see right across the bay from there. I remember often going up there in the daytime. We didn't do any night duty. I think they put a gun emplacement up there eventually.

Previous page: *Groundcrew refuelling an Airspeed Oxford, Wigram.* RNZAF Official, via Air Force Museum, Christchurch, PR2121
Above: *George Judge during his flying training at Ashburton.* George Judge collection

Did you have a uniform?

No, nothing like that. We had an armband and a few rifles that they found, shotguns, .22. I think there was a Lewis gun in the area. We looked at that occasionally and trained on it. Never fired it.

Home Guard armband. ATL, Evening Post Collection, PAColl-8557-47

Who did the training?

I think it was overseen by the Army. It was always at weekends.

I was coming up to 18 and had to fill out the form and be registered. I put a few months on my age and registered early, but they called me up well after I was 18 anyway. Then they sent us to Waiouru for three months' training. The Army was going overseas, but we weren't liable to be sent until we were 21. At that point Japan hadn't come in[to the war], but when Japan came in the situation changed entirely. They held us here as a defence force. It was quite a worry. The Japanese had come down and were almost through in New Guinea at this point. Germany and Italy are way over there, but Japan was coming close, very quickly.

I was keen to get in the Army in New Zealand, at that point. Later on I got a bit tired of the Army. We weren't doing much, only keeping fit by marching. I felt I could do better than the Army, so I volunteered for the Air Force. Then this air liaison business came through and I volunteered for that and got in straight away. The Air Force application was shelved for the time being, probably because they needed us here as a defence force.

How did your parents react?

They didn't mind me being in the local force. I was still around in New Zealand. Dad had been in the First World War and I guess he thought [my involvement] was inevitable. Mum was worried. All mothers are, I think.

> *George recalls his initial compulsory military training in the Territorials at Waiouru with a group of other 18-year-olds from the East Coast.*

Waiouru army camp. ATL, War History Collection, F-19095-1/1

It was basic army training. We went on the range and fired there. Threw grenades. Marched and marched, and froze. It's a cold place, Waiouru, [especially if you are living] in bell tents. We went up in our civilian clothes. We got uniforms — you lined up at the quartermaster's store and he'd look at you and say 'There you are', and bring out something. We never fitted anything. At Waiouru there were no Bren guns. I don't think there was even a sub-machine gun at that point. We had Lewis guns. There weren't too many of them. Like the rifles, they were First World War. They were quite effective.

In a bell tent you had a segment [that was yours]. It came in like a triangle. Rifles were stacked in the centre, out of the way, against the tent pole. There wasn't much room in the tents with all our gear too. When you got frost, the canvas froze solid at night.

How did you find adjusting to the discipline?

That was all right. It depended on your sergeant. Your platoon sergeant was the main one you dealt with. There was an officer, he turned up occasionally. I don't know what he did for the rest of the day. They were Regular Army at Waiouru and their job was to train us. We thought they were tough.

Did you feel patriotic?

At the start it was just an adventure, very much so, but when Japan came in it became pretty serious.

Was that a shock?

To New Zealand, yes — we weren't thinking about Japan. We were caught by surprise. They weren't even thinking of holding a defence force in New Zealand in case Japan came in[to the war].

> *After training George was posted to 1st Hawke's Bay Regiment. After Japan's entry into the war, the Army concentrated on preparing a force for the defence of New Zealand.*

They got the Territorials and all the young fellas in our area into this regiment. When I arrived, they'd settled down at the racecourse in Woodville. We ate under the grandstand. I think the cookhouse was there too. We were in bell tents the whole time I was there.

It was pretty boring. I remember I used to play a lot of cards. That's where I got really brassed off with poker because these older fellas always fleeced me, so I gave that away. Route march — that was the main thing we did. We used to walk up the road from Woodville down towards the Manawatu Gorge one day, and then we'd walk the other way, up towards Dannevirke, the next day. That was our main activity really. It became very boring. It was the best part of a year. We got leave, you could get home, but it was a long journey to Gisborne. You couldn't go home for the weekend.

Woodville was our local. There was a picture theatre there, but I don't think there was even a bus to get there. You had to walk. We were a little way out. I was keen on trout fishing. There were some people I got to know, and I stored my fly-fishing gear at their place and went fishing. I don't recall catching much. I must have had a bike stashed there too.

> *In August 1942, George volunteered for the air liaison section.*

Air liaison section, Palmerston North, George Judge standing, far right. George Judge collection

That section was mainly young fellas, from all round the North Island. There were seven privates and corporals, and a couple of officers.

What did it do?

It liaised with a flight of Royal New Zealand Air Force planes. They were there to reconnoitre and spot against an enemy if we were invaded. We were the Army side that either requested or took information they gave us. We processed the information that they brought back. It'd go back to Army headquarters.

Where was it based?

On Milson aerodrome, by Palmerston North.

How did you hear about it?

They called for volunteers. Notices would go up on the notice board in the 1st Hawke's Bay headquarters at Woodville. I forget where that was — maybe under the grandstand, too. It was all under the grandstand in those days, but it could have been in the stables. We used them, too. Captain Burns was in charge of the headquarters then. He was my teacher at high school, and I think he recommended me.

What made you think you'd like it?

It was Air Force and it was different, and it looked interesting. We lived like the Air Force did, in a hut with bunks. We dined in a dining room. The food was about twice as good as what we'd had in the Army. The Army was very basic. I can remember that if we went out on a route march, they'd dump a few loaves of bread on the breakfast table and you'd cut a few slices and make up your lunch that way.

They might have a bit of cheese, and sometimes there was an apple. There was butter. Breakfast was generally porridge. For tea, you might have boiled eggs and vegies, meat. It was basic, very basic. In the Air Force we used to get scones. They'd bake scones, which was really something.

The RNZAF reconnaissance flight used Hawker Hind aircraft.

The Hawker Hind was a biplane, and reasonably slow. It wasn't the best for that job, but it was the best that New Zealand had at that time. We did a few manoeuvres. We went up Hawera and Wanganui with them; we'd go over the hill to Pahiatua at times. They would practise. We provided maps of a locality for the pilots to look at, and then they'd come back and report their findings.

We had a number of vehicles in that section, and I learnt to drive there in a Morris 10. I had to take two officers over to Pahiatua. They were sitting in the back and I was driving and we hit some fresh metal over the top, going downhill. It was a little hairy until I pulled the vehicle up. It was loose metal — you slide and weave if you're going too fast. I didn't put my brakes on, I just slowed down, and we went quietly from then on. They did comment that flying was a lot safer. We stayed on the road, but it was a bit hairy.

Japan was held at bay. They lost the sea battles [at Coral Sea and Midway] and I think it was becoming obvious that they weren't able to invade New Zealand. The danger had faded, so we were let go home. If you were 21, you were taken into the Army for overseas. That's what happened to some of them in our section, the older ones such as our corporal, Dave Peebles. The officer said, 'They'll rate you down when you go in. Officers are rated down, NCOs are rated down. We'll make you a sergeant.' They were a very nice group to work with.

I came home, it must have been the end of February 1943, and I went back to my old job at Maori Affairs. I worked there for a very short time and my Air Force application caught up with me. They wanted me in the Air Force and I went in, in May 1943.

Where did you go?

I spent a short time in Gisborne. We did guard duty at the aerodrome. The aerodrome was used for training Grumman Avenger pilots. The Avenger was a big torpedo bomber. We were the guard, the ex-Army chaps. There was a bit of fuel there to guard too, I think.

A group of trainee aircrew at a navigation instruction class, Rotorua, c. 1943.
RNZAF Official, via Air Force Museum, Christchurch, PR1950

Were you allowed to live at home?

We had a hut there, but they didn't care where you were as long as you turned up for duty, so it was quite relaxed that way. It was good. They had an underground communication area. It was quite a big thing, and I remember it was still around for years after the war. I think we did the guard on that too. It was operational.

George was then posted to Rotorua for his initial Air Force training.

When we got to Rotorua, we exchanged our Army khaki for Air Force blue. They sorted us out into various categories of aircrew. We had another medical, a very strict one this time. That's where we had the colour-blindness test again.

Why was that important in the Air Force?

It's very important because signals from aerodrome control to aircraft could be sent by signal lamp — there were no radios in training aircraft at this stage. Flares could be used, and these signals were either red or green. A wrong response could be dangerous, or fatal. It's surprising how many people were colour-blind.

We were billeted in tents for a start, then when a course moved out we got into the old hotel, Brents. Everything revolved around Brents. We had our tuition there, and our meals there too.

It could have been there they put us through a compression chamber. That was to check if you could handle the pressure reduction and reducing oxygen as you [gained altitude]. They tested you and eventually they said: you can go for pilot, you can go for navigator, and the chaps who didn't qualify for those, they were air gunners. I chose to be a pilot and made up all sorts of reasons for wanting to be.

A test pilot is fitted with a parachute before a flight in a Tiger Moth at Rongotai, c. 1943.
RNZAF Official, via Air Force Museum, Christchurch, PR1808

We learnt a lot of theory at Rotorua. It was mainly schoolwork.

When you say 'theory' of flying, what did that involve?
It's surprising. The design of the internal combustion engine, aerodynamics, lift, wing loading, et cetera. Meteorology — weather, cloud, and fronts. Then there was elementary navigation. And map-reading, a very essential skill in the air, because you can't stop and ask someone the way while you're flying.

At Ashburton, navigation was easy, with all the rivers flowing from the Alps to the sea. Canada was easy too, with roads all laid out in squares. The railways had large grain silos at each station with the town's name painted in large letters. It was handy if you weren't sure where you were. England was much more difficult, with roads and rail going in all directions and villages and towns all over the place.

After the theory course at Rotorua, George was sent to Ashburton to learn to fly.

What sorts of planes were you training on at Ashburton?
They were Tiger Moths with an open cockpit. Two-seaters.

Tell me about your first time in the plane.
I was apprehensive. Confidence came with skill, later.

Are they good little planes to fly?
They're easy. Very basic, but you can't be ham-handed with them. You have to be very light on the controls.

George recalls his first solo flight.

It's always a surprise, they never tell you. It comes about after eight or ten hours flying with the instructor. With me, he took me up and we did our usual circuit and we came down, and then he undid his harness, got out and said, 'You're on your own.' That's how they did it. There was no building of stress or anything. It was good. It was exhilarating being up on your own.

They had a list of things they had to teach you. They started with the simpler and got more complex. Basically, for a start, they homed in on if you had an engine failure or something went wrong and you had to do a forced landing, and that type of thing. And when we got on the multi-engines [in Canada], what you'd do if one motor stopped.

With the Tiger Moth they trained you if you stalled and spun, but with the Oxford we didn't have any of that. I don't know whether it would have come out of a spin. It was heavier. The Tiger Moth's very forgiving. It's got two wings and plenty of lift, and when I got more practised in England I used to do all sorts of things in it.

I'm just thinking of Ashburton when those big nor'wester winds came through. Did that affect you when you were trying to land?

They didn't fly if it was too bad, but you could go up and within your hour the wind would come up. When you landed — you had to land against the wind — you were almost going backwards. There would be people waiting to grab your wings when you came in so you didn't flip over.

When we'd finished at Ashburton, they sent us home on leave. Just before we went they said, 'You're going to Canada.' Sorted us out then. If you weren't going to Canada, you stayed in New Zealand for training and went to the Pacific. They got into action in the Pacific much quicker than we did, going to Canada. Ours was a longer course.

George went home to Gisborne on his final leave before going to train in Canada as part of the Empire Air Training Scheme.

Where did you leave from?

Auckland. There was no liner for us, it was one of those American Liberty boats. It had brought a cargo out to the Islands, then taken wounded down into Auckland, and there were wounded going back home. About 150 New Zealanders, aircrew, went on that one. We had plenty of room in the holds. It was a cargo boat, a new boat, and virtually its first journey. It didn't have any ballast and she certainly bumped and thumped. It was fast, very fast. I was seasick all the time, with the smell of diesel and new paint. I didn't eat much, I was too sick. I don't travel well in boats.

We each had a watch duty, and had to keep watch for submarines, torpedoes, anything like that. I never saw anything, but sometimes she really speeded up. They opened the throttle and it went, so they had a few frights apparently.

The New Zealanders landed at San Francisco, and then travelled by train into Canada.

I didn't know where I was going at that point, but the sergeant in charge had the list of who was to get off where. We were first off, at Calgary. Sixty of us went to Penhold in Alberta.

The group had to wait about a month while a previous course finished training.

What did you do in that time?
We visited Red Deer and walked around, went ice skating. I think there were dances. On that aerodrome there was a canteen, there was a YMCA, and all the facilities for recreation. You could play ping-pong.

Group of trainee pilots on the Empire Air Training Scheme, Penhold, Alberta. George Judge is third from right. George Judge collection

What was the countryside like?
It was very flat, running into scrub. It was like manuka, that type of thing. Around the aerodrome was all barren wasteland, really. It was starting to rise to the Rockies.

What were the people like?
They were very friendly, very good to us. The first day we were walking down the street and an older man came up and invited us to his home. From then on, if we were in town we could go to the home. They had two girls at home and a young boy.

George was training on Airspeed Oxford aircraft.

It had been designed as a light bomber, and it was used for multi-engine training by the British. All the personnel were British there — the instructors, planes, everything was British.

What was the difference between the Tiger Moths and the Oxford?
The Oxford was a lot bigger, heavier, steadier. It was a very stable plane to fly. And faster, quite a lot faster.

George trained at Penhold from March to August 1944. He recalls his only accident.

The planes they used at night were always a bit rough. Your battery wasn't too good, your lights weren't very bright, things like that. I got off the runway. It was after the thaw, wet and muddy, and I got stuck and couldn't get back on the runway. I got one wheel off and it was stuck. Someone came up behind me and stopped. I thought, Well, that's good, he's seen me. I didn't have many lights showing and it was wet

George, on ground, gopher-shooting on a Canadian prairie. The woman is a member of the family with whom he spent time in Red Deer. George Judge collection

and drizzly. I thought he'd seen me. I was just going to get out — you're not supposed to leave your plane while the motor's running, but I was going to get out and thump on his door to tell him I was there — then he started off. He chewed my wing tip off. They had a bit of an enquiry, but there was nothing either of us could do on a night like that.

At the end of the course we got our wings. That was good. It was what we had all aimed for.

George then travelled by train across Canada and by ship to Scotland.

We went by rail from Scotland down to Brighton. New Zealand headquarters was there for aircrew. The Grand Hotel was for NCOs, and the officers had another smaller hotel somewhere that they used. All the beaches were barbed-wired.

We went out to elementary flying schools. Basically it was learning to map-read your way round England and keep your flying skill. We stayed there for a month or two, sometimes longer. We were back to flying Tiger Moths. When they'd checked us out, we'd take navigators and they'd practise navigating their way round. They had more aircrew than they needed at this point. They hadn't had the losses that they expected.

Were you disappointed?
We were, yes.

What about leave?
We got a bit of leave. I went up to Edinburgh; I had a cousin and an aunt up there, and I stayed with them. I went salmon fishing with my uncle up the loch and caught one or two fish. Brighton's only a little over an hour or so from London by fast train. London was pretty quiet. There was a lot of bomb damage. All the troops were over in Europe.

There was still the threat of attack by German V1 and V2 rockets.

You couldn't do much about it. I think they just came to accept it, the constant fear. We walked around. We'd stay somewhere and then we'd look at the sights, see the buildings.

George (front left) with other New Zealanders in the United Kingdom, c. 1945.
George Judge collection

Did you realise that the war was coming to an end?

Oh, yes. They were held up by the winter, but as soon as the spring came they started to move, and they moved fast. We'd been away from home for a while, and I think a lot of us were looking forward to coming back home again.

George went to London to celebrate on VE Day, 8 May 1945.

Every Tom, Dick and Harry that lived there was out in the street. A lot of Army, Navy, Air Force, everyone. All congregated in London if you were near enough. We stayed the night there. We got leave, I think they just let us go. We drank a lot and there was singing. They'd get together and sing, in hotels and the wide open.

After VE Day, what did you do then?

They still had Japan to deal with. Some of our boys who went into the Fleet Air Arm were training still, but they just held us. We didn't do much flying, and then we started to help out with the harvest in the autumn. We'd go out for the day, stook up grain and pitchfork it up into the wagons and stack. Lovely weather in the south of England. Then we were waiting to be shipped home. We were at Brighton.

George explains how he felt about the use of atomic bombs against Japan.

If it was going to get the war over, we were quite happy. America had to land in Japan, and we knew that they'd have to fight for every inch of it, and it saved a tremendous lot of soldiers' lives.

Not long afterwards, George returned by ship to New Zealand.

Went to Wellington and eventually we got home on the railway. The railway had gone right through to Gisborne by then.

What was that like, seeing your family again after all that time?
Good. Good. Seeing friends, going fishing again too.

George returned to work at the Maori Affairs Department, but found it difficult to settle back into civilian life after his war service.

I bought a small piece of land and got out onto the land. I had a small orchard, citrus mainly.

Many of us had virtually gone from high school straight into the services. I started drinking there, as many of us did. I dropped that, fortunately, many years ago. In Canada, alcohol was rationed and you had to be over 21, but we managed to get around that. It was boredom, because we didn't do much reading. Many took up smoking, that was the norm. We even had an issue of American cigarettes in England.

You learn a lot of good habits in the Air Force, and I often think I'm a better driver for it. You look around a lot, eyes open all the time.

George met his wife, June Mackay, while he was working in the Maori Affairs Department, and the couple married in 1951.

Troops arrive back in New Zealand. ATL, John Pascoe Collection, F-1637-1/4

Do you go to Anzac Day parades?

I do now, yes. I didn't have much to do with the parades for many years, because fortunately few of my friends lost their lives. Over the years the ranks have thinned, and I go now to give support and in appreciation for the real sacrifices so many men made, and which I was spared.

'SWORN TO
SECRECY'

Betty van PRAAG, W1228,
Leading Aircraftwoman, WAAF

Betty Tossman was born in Wellington in 1922, the daughter of Philip and Olga Tossman, who had emigrated to New Zealand before the First World War. The family was Jewish and was extremely worried about the situation in Europe during the 1930s.

Do you think you were aware that a war was going to come?

Oh yes, oh yes. My parents were very politically-minded people. Politics were discussed freely and often in our household. Oh yes, we knew that.

We didn't have a personal involvement of our own flesh and blood as far as we knew, although I later discovered that many of my father's extended family whom we never knew were eliminated by the Germans in Russia. Jewish people began to arrive here from Germany and Austria, and it was a wake-up call here, I can tell you. There was much gathering around and helping other Jewish people, which got mixed in eventually with the war effort, and knitting socks for soldiers, and balaclavas, all of that. Everybody was filled with doom and gloom.

When she left Wellington East Girls' College, Betty studied at Gilbey's Business College before beginning work with an accountancy firm in Wellington. She then became secretary to the manager of Twentieth Century Fox in New Zealand. In 1941, she was one of the first 10 young women to enlist in the Women's Auxiliary Air Force.

Previous page: *WAAFs on parade in Wellington, c. 1943.* RNZAF Official, via Air Force Museum, Christchurch, PR1148
Above: *Betty Tossman.* Betty van Praag collection
Opposite: *A WAAF modelling the uniform.* ATL, Gordon Burt Collection, F-36400-1/2

Tell me why you decided to enlist in the Air Force.

Now that is something that I've asked myself over and over again. I don't know. It was new, and Twentieth Century Fox was not particularly stimulating. It was there to do, and so I did it. When I joined the Air Force there was no women's Navy or Army force. I had a rush of patriotic blood to the head, and that was why I did it, I suppose. No friends came with me. My brother was in the Air Force. Perhaps that was an influence.

Can you remember whether you discussed it with your parents?

Yes, I would have discussed it in full. In those days, at age 17 or 18 you did not move without the permission of your parents. That was generally so. They were quite proud of me, and they were pleased.

It was quite a process, because it was at the very, very beginning and there were no official guidelines. I went to Air Department to enlist, and then I had to be filtered through by the police. I can remember going to the police station. They took my fingerprints. I had to have people recommend me. Among the people serving at that time was Charles Weinstein, a well-known businessman in Wellington. He was a flight lieutenant and adjutant of Air Department, and he was happy to facilitate my entry, and ease my way.

I had to have several character references, but I was acceptable. And I went in with the first few women. There were about eight or ten of us. We had no numbers, we had no uniform, we didn't have anything. It was winter and we were sent out to Rongotai. There I went and was mustered into the equipment section. I did shorthand and typing, working in the office. I was secretary to the adjutant of the equipment section.

What did the equipment section do?

It was a store, and it was one of those big, big buildings left over from the Wellington Exhibition. They were huge, they were cold, and they were draughty. The wind whistled through them. We were given a blanket to wrap around ourselves because it was so cold. We had no uniforms, and every hour or so they would muster us outside and we'd walk or run around the building to get warm and then come back to our office desks and wrap our blankets around ourselves. It was very basic.

What about the men? How did they react to having women there?
Oh God, they'd be delighted. What do you think? Rude? No. Jealous? No. We were the butt of some fun, jokes, but that was it. Everybody was polite and courteous.

This aerial view was taken while the Centennial Exhibition buildings were under construction in 1939. ATL, W.H. Raine Collection, F-19697-1/4

Practical jokes?
I can recall being sent along to the stores department. The sergeant said, 'Go and get a two-inch or three-quarter inch', or some measurement, 'bastard file.' The thought of saying 'bastard' was so — it was almost impossible for me to say. I had a very sheltered upbringing and that was not one of the current words in the family. But I did manage to say that and everybody in the equipment section, the young men, collapsed with laughter at a young girl coming and asking for that. These days it would mean absolutely nothing, but in those days it was extremely embarrassing for me.

Eventually Betty got her uniform.

The day arrived when I had a skirt and a jacket, hat, shoes and stockings, shirts. Then we were taught to march. Off we went with people getting us in order. The berets were all right. They came in a little later. We had inspection in the morning and were told to shine our buttons if they weren't shone, and so on. We always wore make-up. We weren't wearing earrings much — women didn't have pierced ears. You could wear a watch, and I suppose a wedding ring or an engagement ring, but I'm sure that would be it.

The WAAF drum and fife band leads a WAAF parade at Rongotai. Betty van Praag collection

The thing that gave me amusement was the drum and fife band. I was asked if I would join, and I thought I'd love to. Anything to keep you outside and do something a little different. I was a drummer. We had a side drum and gauntlets and braid, and tassels hanging down from the braid, and things that went swish hanging in front of the drums. It was lovely.

I enjoyed it very, very much. It was good fun. We'd go over at lunchtime for rehearsals at the lower part of a big square surrounded by the old Rongotai buildings left over from the Exhibition. There must have been 20 or more WAAFs in the band. We had a line-up of drums, five or six, maybe eight drummers, and the drum major was a tall, willowy, blonde girl, a lovely girl. The fife players came at the back.

There were parades through town of units going overseas — not necessarily Air Force, sometimes Army or Navy. Anzac Days. In wartime, I would guess that it was any excuse for a parade, for a little bit of morale building. People stood and watched and cheered. We paraded ahead of the wonderful Air Force band — it's still a wonderful band — and the troops following after. Perhaps they put us there so the troops couldn't hear us very well, because it was not a good band. Even as drum and fife bands go, it wasn't. It would not have attracted attention for its beautiful music.

While Betty enjoyed the drum and fife band, she appreciated the discipline that went with being in the Air Force less.

You just had to do what you were told. I found that extremely difficult to adjust to. My brother was seven years older than I, so I was almost an only child, and that kind of senseless discipline was very hard

WAAFs plot aircraft movements at the Central Group Headquarters fighter operations room. RNZAF Official, via Air Force Museum, Christchurch, PR3771

to take. I took it because I had no choice. It was not the sort of thing where you said, 'I'll hand in my notice and go and work for somebody else now.' You couldn't do that.

After her time in the equipment section and in headquarters at Rongotai, Betty was transferred to Air Force Central Group Headquarters, which was located in the basement of the Dominion Museum in Buckle Street in Wellington.

They had rooms under there, which I suppose had been storage rooms, and which were taken over by the Air Force. At Central Group, we had what were known as operations rooms, and there we could plot aircraft coming and going, and the movements of ships. We had cipher rooms, which sent and received enciphered messages. There were sections set up for wireless, so we had a finger on the pulse of what was going on. It was a top-secret job at the time, and we didn't talk about it. We just didn't. You were sworn to secrecy, and the information that you had in your head was secret information that you didn't divulge. Not under any circumstances.

I can remember my father, who belonged to the Home Guard, getting ready for an emergency exercise which we had planned in our office: over this coming weekend the sirens will go at that time and the emergency will last until that time. It had been advertised, so everybody knew it was coming, but nobody knew when. My father had got his uniform ready — which was an armband — and he and Mr Murphy next door were trying to get the information out of me. They needed to know whether or not to take a hip flask when the emergency siren went off, and I simply couldn't tell them. I was not able to. They were not best pleased with me, but I couldn't help it. But they were well-equipped when the siren went off. They went right to their post, down in Kilbirnie Crescent, and did what the Home Guard did. There was quite a lot, I think, of going to the hip flask.

We knew what was happening. We knew that there were submarines in Cook Strait. There were posts set up all around New Zealand where people, residents around the coast, kept an eye out for ships and unusual movements. They were officially doing that job for us, for the country. It was interesting, some of it has not been told to this day.

When I first went there, under the museum there was much digging out of solid concrete walls and brick. Diggers and drivers and things, hacking, banging. It was a very noisy place. There was one gentleman who would pull us up for undoing the top button of our jacket. Now that was fashionable, because the fighter pilots left the top button of their jacket undone. That's how you knew they were fighter pilots. And we WAAFs liked to walk around with the top button of our jacket undone because it was trendy. We would be pulled up. All this clatter in the corridor, and the officer would be screaming at you, 'Do up the button of your jacket!' The noise would suddenly stop and he was left screaming in the total silence. It was funny.

What did you do there?

The same sort of thing. I was secretary to the Air Commodore Commanding, Air Commodore Findlay. He was a gorgeous man. There was a wing commander from England, Johnny Hill, and some New Zealand guys. They were good men. They were really, really good at what they did. It was a great contrast to Rongotai, where little was done and much was made of nothing.

Johnny had fought in the Battle of Britain. Why was he transferred here? I suppose to set up Central Group. He'd finished his tour of duty. These were men who had done dangerous things, so they were easy to work for because they knew what was going on, they knew where they stood with life.

We used to march outside sometimes, and be mustered out to do a march here or there. By that time I'd been promoted, so I could take the marching group, but there wasn't much of that. Discipline, as such, wasn't necessary, because everybody was disciplined who was there, and if you weren't disciplined, you didn't stay very long.

Was it a secret that you were there, or did everybody know?

I just worked up at the museum. Everybody knew that there was some Army or Air Force activity there, and that's where I worked. I did office work, that's all. But what was in there was not to be spoken about. There was a Northern Group and a Southern Group also, and we were in direct communication by telephone, Morse code, radio, and whatever devices were 'state of the art' for those days.

Frances Kain was the WAAF Superintendent from 1941 until 1943, when she was succeeded by Elsie Carlyon.

Mrs Kain was way above me in the stratosphere. She was at headquarters and I had very little to do with her. I saw her, and I think she might have spoken to me once or twice. In my mind she was a little woman, with dark hair. Mrs Carlyon was another matter altogether. She was gorgeous. She was well-liked, and for a very good reason. She was an extremely fine woman. Carried a smile with her. She was a lovely woman, absolutely. She was blonde, round-faced and a rounder lady than Mrs Kain. I saw more of her, and when we saw each other we knew each other's names. She had a lovely way with her and we liked each other.

Betty does not recall being given any information about contraception or venereal disease when she joined the WAAFs.

Are you joking? No. The short answer is no. We had no sex education whatsoever.

The Air Force was just hoping you'd all behave yourselves?
Yes — hoping against hope, I would say. One or two girls became pregnant. We knew who they were, and we knew that they had left and they were under a cloud. It was a very, very different life. The Pill had not yet been invented and other forms of contraception were whispered about. 'Contraceptive' was a bit of a dirty word. I think it was a bit worse than 'bastard'. On the scale of bad, it was pretty bad. There was a reason to remain virginal.

What about when the American troops came to town, then?
There was huge excitement. I can remember the day they arrived. Saturday. We lived on Evans Bay Road and we heard this tramp, tramping. It was loud, and it got louder. Then it got very loud and I rushed to the window to have a look. And there were, I don't know, four or six wide, hundreds of Americans marching. It was an astonishing sight. We didn't expect anything like that. They were all mustering on the Kilbirnie

US troops arrive in Wellington, 1942.
ATL, War History Collection, F-32267-1/4

recreation ground, and within five minutes we had American Marines knocking on the door and saying, 'Could we use the phone, ma'am?' They were telephoning and getting taxis and rushing off into town.

That was when the fun started in Wellington, actually. It was lovely. Some came to Rongotai. We marched for them. We played 'Marching Through Georgia', not realising it was politically incorrect to do so. The Americans were good-looking, for the most part. They were, almost without exception, well-mannered. They had far more money than any Kiwi soldier. We found that it wasn't a matter of 'Come out on Saturday night, we'll go to the pictures' — a lovely Kiwi guy picking you up and taking you in the tramcar and reading the *Sports Post* at halftime while you licked an ice cream, and then going home on the tram. It wasn't like that any more. We were picked up in taxis, and we went to dances. By then I was a little older and I didn't have to ask my mother's permission quite so much. We had a lot of fun. Town was crowded with Americans. They loved it here. Some were hopelessly made the fall guy — they were overcharged for things, all that stuff.

They brought flowers and chocolates. Oh yes, oh yes. A corsage and a box of chocolates. Very often the chocolates were for your mother. Mothers loved the Marines. They were so charming. Dad would be offered petrol coupons.

Were they well-behaved?

As far as I'm concerned, I didn't meet any that were not. They'd try it on all right, but everybody did that, everybody. Men did that. We were continually fighting off hands, many hands, all the time. We had no legal protection against that. It was accepted. It wasn't acceptable, but it was accepted. I didn't like it a bit: don't do that, it's not welcome.

Particularly if it was a superior officer, then you had a little problem. If you worked for a guy who was trying it on, it really could be quite awkward. You didn't complain, you either put up with it or put an end to it the best way you could, but nobody would continue to pester you if you made it quite clear at minute one. And it would stop if you were firm enough.

Were you able to do that?

I was able to do that quite well.

Betty recalls the defensive tactics of her friend Olga.

She let an officer kiss her and she kissed his collar. Off he went with a big lipstick mark on his collar. He didn't try that again with her.

In terms of the newspapers, were people kept up to date with what was going on?

I think so. We were bombarded with propaganda, and I only knew what was going on in terms of the forces in New Zealand.

I think one knew one was being bombarded with propaganda, but we had to accept it because it was all there was. There was no internet then.

One thing that I do remember very clearly was hearing on the BBC long strings of strange-sounding words. You'd tune to the BBC at certain hours and they'd be saying things like 'Mayflower. Sheep will arrive at two. Brick-coloured handbag', and so on. These were secret things they were saying to people in Europe. There'd be five or ten minutes of code. So you knew there was stuff going on.

Dance band performing at the Majestic Cabaret, Wellington. Note the US and NZ flags decorating the backdrop.
ATL, E.M. Alderdice Collection, C16006

Did it ever occur to you that the Allies wouldn't win?

No, not for a moment. We knew the war was going badly, but Winston Churchill was there — how could anything go wrong? Everybody felt like that. The man was an absolute inspiration. His past history was long forgotten. He absolutely won that war with his speaking, he was brilliant. No, we had no doubt about that. It never occurred to me for one moment — even if the Japs had invaded here. But there was a feeling of it being just day to day: we got through today, all right, let's hope tomorrow will be OK.

Americans were pouring in here, then they were disappearing. Then we'd read about invasions in Guadalcanal or wherever it was. It was these guys.

Betty recalls that VJ Day was wild in Brisbane. The state of the street shows that there were great celebrations in Wellington, too. ATL, John Pascoe Collection, F-1825-1/4

Was there ever any possibility of you going overseas?

I was asked to go to Fiji. Central Group wanted me to go over there. I was dying to go, I was aching to go, but my mother wouldn't let me.

My mother and father would not permit me to go, and in hindsight they were probably right. They said absolutely not, so I didn't go. I got engaged to an American instead.

Betty was transferred to Northern Group Headquarters in Auckland for a short time, but her health deteriorated. She was told by her specialist that she had a congenital heart murmur, and that she had to leave the Air Force. She was given an honourable discharge, and became engaged to Solomon Dichter, a US Marine in the 2 Marine Division. After her discharge, Betty went to Brisbane to visit her aunt. Dichter was there, and the couple married. Soon after, Dichter was posted to the Pacific. Betty was in Brisbane on VE and VJ Days.

They were a couple of very wild nights. VJ Day was particularly wild. We celebrated it at Lennon's Hotel in Brisbane, which was then opposite the river. We went with all our buddies, and a fine old time was had by all. We had much to celebrate.

After Dichter went to the Pacific, Betty met Jim van Praag, a pilot in the Dutch forces, at that time based in Brisbane. She subsequently divorced Dichter and married Jim van Praag in New York in 1946. She recalls hearing news about the concentration camps at the end of the war.

That was quite unbelievable. By then I had met Jim's parents, and they had family that was still in the Netherlands and Belgium. The van Praag home had been taken over in Antwerp as officers' quarters, and now I knew, and was related to, people who had been directly involved in this. That put a very different complexion on it. It made the whole thing much more personal, and much more traumatic and disgusting. The first time I saw pictures of the concentration camps was back here in Wellington at the Majestic Theatre. I saw those pictures of the bodies and the horror, and that made a deep impression on me. I never want to see that again. I've seen it now, it's in there. I could see that picture a thousand times and it couldn't make a deeper impression. It still means the same to me. Beyond belief. Disgusting. Dreadful. And now I know people who have numbers tattooed on their arms and who have been through some of that horror.

Betty reflects on the long-term effects of her time as a WAAF.

I think it made me more independent and self-reliant. It sure did that. You got out more, and mixed with all kinds of people from all kinds of places. I loved that. So there was that about it, which I enjoyed. What I didn't like was being herded. One thing: I'll never wear Air Force blue again.

Did you feel it was your duty?
Yes, I did. I did. We were all flushed with patriotism then. There's nothing wrong with patriotism.

Now that I have a son and grandsons, war seems a total, utter, endless obscenity. Let the politicians get together, let them find some way of sorting out problems, but war of people on people, human beings on human beings, is an obscenity. Nobody wins. Nobody. Perhaps the arms manufacturers . . .

'ALL
DEDICATED
GIRLS'

Maisie MUNRO, W13, Petty Officer Telegraphist, WRNZNS

Maisie Hoskin was among the first intake of women into the WRNZNS. She was born in Petone, near Wellington, in September 1922. Her parents had met and married in Canterbury after the First World War before moving north, and Maisie was their only child. Marian Hoskin had been a dressmaker before her marriage, and Maisie's father Barton was a carpenter.

HE WENT TO the First World War and was wounded somewhere in France. He had a crippled hand and it used to cause him a lot of pain. He'd often get me to rub it at nights. Poor thing. He was a carpenter and it affected his work. It gradually got a little better as the years went by, but it was a while before he was able to get right back into carpentry again.

Maisie attended school in Petone, and then trained at Gilbey's Business College in Wellington. After leaving Gilbey's she worked in the office at the W.T. Rawleigh Company — the home of the travelling 'Rawleigh's Man'. She does not remember knowing much about the international situation before war was declared, but joined the Women's War Service Auxiliary when it was established in July 1940.

My father was one of the first five Scouts in New Zealand in Kaiapoi, in the Weka Patrol, and somebody knew of his interest in signals, so he was asked to take about 18 girls in the Women's War Service Auxiliary

Previous page: *Wrens on parade at HMS* Philomel.
Royal New Zealand Navy Museum, ABY0100
Above: *Petty Officer Maisie Hoskin.* Maisie Munro collection
Right: *New Plymouth members of the Women's War Service Auxiliary ambulance unit on parade.*
Joan Court-Patience collection

and train them in all branches of signalling. I went along too. That was in our spare time; we all had our daytime jobs. We went up to the Hutt Rec, once a week, and learnt all about signalling.

What sorts of signals?

Flags, lamps, Morse key, semaphore. We had a pretty good grounding. After that, I went into the Wrens. It was something that we heard about, and people were being put into factories to do war work. When I heard about the Wrens, I thought yes, that'd be the thing. I'll try to get in. After several interviews I was accepted. Even a detective interviewed me, he wanted to know all about my family. Anyway, I was accepted, they took me and gave me my number, 13, and that was the beginning of it.

My Dad was thrilled about it, because he'd always wanted to join the Navy, but for some reason if you were from Kaiapoi it had to be the Army. Mum was a bit doubtful, she had to get used to it.

> *Maisie was in the first group of 20 Wrens, and, although not all were put into signals, most were telegraphists.*

We went to Navy Office for six weeks, supposedly six weeks' training, but we already had to be able to send and receive 22 words a minute, so it was just for them to see exactly what we could do.

> *Maisie lived at home.*

Some of the girls came from other parts of the country and they lived in a Wrens' hostel in Wellington. We had a sort of a uniform. It was navy blue, but it was very plain and dowdy. It got spruced up as we went along — skirt and jacket and hat, and grey lisle stockings, black shoes, grey gloves.

Miss Herrick was the Director of Wrens. I think I must have met her, she must have been one of my initial interviewers. She was also a great Girl Guide. Helen

Ruth Herrick. Royal New Zealand Navy Museum, APD0002

Fenwick was the next in line. She was a sweet thing. I didn't really meet them much, because once you were on the job you were nowhere near them.

I was a 'Probationary Wren' to start with. I think that was for three months, and then 'Wren' — 'Telegraphist', of course, attached to that. And then, 'Leading Wren Telegraphist', when we went up to ZLP on Tinakori Hill. I did six weeks at Navy Office and then went up to ZLP. It was a small building, half Post Office and half Navy. We learnt what it was like to watch-keep, what it was like to be a telegraphist. It was run by the naval ratings, petty officers, so they were telling us what to do. They were a bit doubtful about us, I think. I don't think at that stage they fully realised that we were there to do a job and to release them to go to sea. One person in particular was really bad. He was sarcastic to us and it was really quite difficult to cope with, but we had to.

> *Maisie and her colleagues were receiving messages in code from naval stations overseas which were then sent to the Navy Office.*

We had early wireless sets, nothing like what we struck when we went to Waiouru.

> *The Wrens had to work at night as there were four watches each day.*

I never got used to watch-keeping. I never got too good at the early morning watch, I was always too tired. They had arranged a room with a couple of mattresses on the floor, and when we came off watch at night we were able to sleep there.

> *Maisie spent a year at ZLP and was then transferred to station ZLO at Waiouru, where she worked for two years.*

The WAAFs had been in what we called the Wrennery. I don't know where they went, but they went somewhere else and we took over. It was about seven miles away from the Army camp. The radio mechanics in the Navy were about five miles away, and in the other direction was Taihape.

> *Maisie enjoyed living in the Wrennery, where there were four Wrens to a cabin.*

It was good. I think we were pretty sensible about it. They were all dedicated girls who were doing what they wanted to do, and I think that makes a big difference. I'm still in touch with some of the girls.

There were eight staff in the galley to prepare the meals.

Meals were very good, very nourishing. When we were on night watch and therefore off in the mornings, we'd all get together and go down and peel vegies, carrots and potatoes.

We had to scrub the floors and be ready for the inspection every week. It was run like a naval establishment, which it was.

Who would do those inspections?
The commanding officer and the Wren officer. They would come round together and inspect us, make sure everything was shipshape. There wasn't much furniture, just our bunks and our tallboys — there was nothing much to collect dust by the time we'd scrubbed the floors.

What was it like in the winter up there?
Cold, very cold. I suppose we got used to it to a certain degree. It was perhaps just as well that my mother and father didn't let me have a hot-water bottle at home, because I wasn't conditioned to too much warmth in bed. We had greatcoats. While we were up there, we were issued with bell-bottom trousers and jerseys, scarves and mittens — everything that you need when it's cold.

From her hut to where Maisie worked at the receiving station was about a 20-minute walk.

We went across paddocks, trudging through the snow. We worked

Maisie Hoskin at Waiouru with her future husband, Rex Randall.
Maisie Munro collection

in a big building with a kitchen and another office that the Chief Petty Officer used, and the petty officers' office. There was one room that housed all the telegraphists on their different skeds, working Australia and Canada, and Bombay and England. We had a Creed machine, which was like a manual typewriter, with the tape of messages it received coming out the side in Morse dots and dashes. This tape was then transmitted on to the operators at the other end by feeding it through another machine.

There was always a male petty officer in charge, and a Wren petty officer, and a leading telegraphist. It altered as time went by. There were only about three or four girls — Wrens — in the beginning, but it gradually built up until there were seven or eight on each watch.

In the receiving room at ZLO, Waiouru.
Maisie Munro collection

The Wrens worked on a wireless set wearing headphones, receiving messages in Morse which they wrote down as they arrived.

The Morse code signals came in groups of five, so you didn't know what was coming, any more than you knew what you were sending. The Morse messages went to the teleprinter office, which was connected to Wellington. There was always a Wren teleprinter operator. The messages all went down to Wellington, to Navy Office, and they had decoders and people that handled that end of it. We did our job and they did theirs.

They also sent messages.

You had your Morse key at your right hand. The messages came from Navy Office. It was all very hush-hush. We were allowed to [talk about what we did], but there wasn't much to tell.

We got some leave, but it was a bit of a problem at Waiouru. There was a rail strike at one stage so we didn't get off-station for a long time, but otherwise we got leave now and then. We'd go for a weekend, always on the train.

Did you get leave to go into Taihape?

Depending on our watch, yes. That was quite good, we liked that. We'd go and have lunch for a change, and take our collars into the Chinese laundry to have them cleaned. They did a beautiful job of them and they always came back all white and shiny. We could never have done them like that, at least I couldn't. We had starched collars. We got a lot of collars because that was the dirtiest thing, your neck. There was no such thing as a shirt with a collar attached. Taihape wasn't a very big place, I think it had largely farming people. We didn't get in very often, but it was good. We'd have a big sing-song in the back of the truck coming home. We had good Wren drivers, they were marvellous.

We had a good drying room, but as time went by there was less and less room because we got more and more Wrens. We had a clothesline too, outside, but that wasn't always successful, because if you forgot and left your shirt out overnight when it was wintertime you could stand it up on the ground when you took it off. It would be frozen. We had a YMCA, which was very good. We could get morning and afternoon teas there, and they had a table tennis table.

There were also dances.

I didn't go to those very often. You couldn't always reckon on going to these functions — not that there were that many — because it would depend on which watch you were on.

Off-duty Wrens at Waiouru.
Maisie Munro collection

A little dog turned up at one stage. I don't know where it came from. It was supposedly Miss Chesney's dog, but it wasn't there for long. A pet lamb turned up, but that too grew up. We weren't allowed pets. Miss Chesney was our Wren supervisor; she was in charge of the Wrens up there. She was nice. She was very pleasant, actually. We all respected her tremendously. I think the only time we had a sort of a mutiny was when it was decided that we were to take it in turns polishing her shoes. The girls sat down and wouldn't do it, so they gave that up.

Was there anybody who people didn't like?

No, I don't think so. We were all our own persons, and you got to know what people were like. I suppose that's like any job. Even if you didn't altogether approve of them, you had to like them. You had no choice.

The powers that be decided we had to sit a petty officers' exam. There was a lot to learn and it was a case of study whenever you could, and watch-keep at the same time. It was all signalling rules and regulations and instructions. I think I learnt two great big tomes by heart. Five of us passed, but they only wanted four petty officer telegraphists at that time.

What happened to the other one?

She just remained a leading Wren. It was a bit sad.

There were petty officers' quarters down the other end of the Wrennery, so, instead of sharing with three others, I shared with one other. We had our own sitting room and fireplace.

Did you have a different uniform as a petty officer?

No, but we changed badges and buttons from black buttons to gilt buttons. We had the telegraphist's badge on the right arm. When you're a leading Wren you had an anchor on your left arm, and when you became a petty officer you had crossed anchors.

We were made petty officers in the commanding officer's office, and then we had to go straight down to the quartermaster's, where you got the bits and pieces of your uniform, and pick up our new badges and buttons, and go back to the Wrennery and change it all over. We weren't allowed to come out until we'd done that.

The unfortunate thing was that the girl who passed the exam but wasn't wanted at that stage was sharing my cabin. She just lay there and looked down, and she said, 'I guess I'll just have to write and tell my mother that she won't have a daughter with gilt buttons.' It was hard.

Maisie was engaged when she went to Waiouru.

What was your fiancé's name?

Ron Baird. He was a sergeant in the Army. He was killed in the Pacific, on Mono Island, by a Japanese sniper. It was a bit difficult, but Miss Chesney was so lovely to me at that time. I remember that night, about 11 o'clock, I was sound asleep. All of a sudden there was Miss Chesney looking at me and saying that Ron had been killed and I had to get up. They were taking me to the station to go home. She was so nice.

I had a week's leave. I went back and carried on, but I think I must have been a bit of a trial to my friends at that time. It was a time to get through.

> *After the war, Maisie visited Ron's grave at Bourail cemetery in New Caledonia, run by the Commonwealth War Graves Commission. Maisie recalls that, although during the war she did not like the Germans, she had much stronger feelings about the Japanese. Maisie describes her attitude towards the latter during the war.*

I hated the Japanese, really hated them. I thought they were a cruel people. They were different people from us, completely. So were the Germans, but somehow the Japs were worse. I suppose that's because they were closer to home.

Did people think they were going to invade New Zealand?
Yes, we did. They got close enough to it. They got to Australia.

What about American troops, did you have anything to do with them?
No. At the time we were doing our six-week course at Navy Office, my father gave me a long hatpin to carry in my bag, because we heard stories about girls being raped and all the rest of it. He said, 'Just stick it in. They won't worry you any more.' We didn't see much of them because we were too busy working. It was only to-ing and fro-ing in the streets that you ever saw them.

> *Maisie describes the role of the so-called 'Fu' operators at the receiving station at Waiouru.*

I think there were only about four of them, all men, and they listened in on Japanese signals. They were nice, quiet guys; they just did their job. We didn't have anything to do with it.

Did you get to know people's Morse?
I didn't, because I was a petty officer. It's one of those things — you're good at your job and you get promotion so you find you're not doing it, but a lot of the girls got to know the men on the other

ZLO, Waiouru. Royal New Zealand Navy Museum, ACB0139

end. They got quite chatty. They could say things like 'Your Morse is good', or something personal. It was nice.

As a petty officer, Maisie had a supervisory role.

I didn't get to operate after that, just be there with the male petty officer. I taped a lot of the Creed things. I worked it out for myself what to do. Before that, a leading Wren was in the same position. After we studied and passed the petty officer's exam, we were still doing the same thing.

I wasn't there for the end of the Japanese war. I got married in January 1945 and three or four months later I found I was pregnant. My leading Wren, Sue, was very good to me. It was a bit difficult getting up — part of my duties was to get up early on the two o'clock watch and wake the girls, because everybody was sound asleep. I found that a bit difficult because I wasn't always feeling very well. So Sue said, 'I'll do that for you', and all I had to do was get myself onto watch. That was all right until the CO found out about it, and he said that it was my job and that was that. I got a discharge on compassionate grounds a couple of months later, I suppose. I had to go to Shelly Bay, where the naval establishment was. There was a doctor and he made sure I was pregnant. Then that was that.

Where did you go after that?

I came home, home to my mother, because my husband, Rex Randall, was in the Navy still. And I waited. Then the Japanese war finished in August, and Rex got his discharge after that and he came home to my mum too. I had my son in December. We got a telegram from the CO — well, he wasn't our CO by then, as we'd all finished. It said, 'Will he be a sparker?' Because that's what they knew the telegraphists as: sparkers.

What was it like being a civilian again?

I was busy having my baby, but it was a bit of a shock. No more war, no more telegraphy, or anything. But everybody was on the move. There were several of my old colleagues getting married.

We put in for a state house and got a state flat which nowadays I believe is in a very run-down area of Petone, but they were very nice. There were two bedrooms, and it was brand new, so we were pretty lucky. Then we decided to buy a section and build our own place. At least, we didn't build it ourselves, but my dad built it for us in Korokoro.

Maisie and Rex got an ex-serviceman's rehabilitation loan to buy the section.

Except it didn't count for me, because I was a woman, I suppose. If I'd been by myself, I could have had it, but I was married and he was getting it.

Maisie and Rex also had a daughter. Maisie married her second husband, Bob Munro, in 1966. Now a widow, she lives in Lower Hutt. She reflects on her time as a Wren.

I think it made me grow up, I really do. I think it was the making of me, because I learnt to live with other people, to know that there was a war on. Staying at home couldn't have done that. It was a special part of life, and the girls that I knew then and that I still keep in touch with, I think we all feel the same. It was a special little time that belongs to all of us.

'I WANTED A DRIVING JOB'

Ngaire GIBBONS, w816192, Corporal, WAAC

When Ngaire Lawrence enlisted in the Women's Auxiliary Army Corps in 1942, she was able to fulfil her wish to become a driver. Born in Feilding in 1921, she grew up with her younger brother on the farm of their parents, Boyne and Vera Lawrence, near Sanson. Ngaire boarded at Solway College in Masterton and then returned home to help on the farm. She joined the St John Ambulance, and after war was declared in 1939 used to ride her bike to Feilding to take part in St John's training.

T HERE WAS ANOTHER GIRL up in that area and we used to bike seven miles into Feilding. We manned a truck — we had our heavy transport licences — that was used as an ambulance.

When did you learn to drive?

I first learnt to drive a car when I was 10, on the farm. We used to put lumps of wood out in the paddock, and I learnt to back through them and all that sort of caper. I'd been driving for ages until somebody mentioned to Dad about me driving when they knew I didn't have a licence, so he made an appointment for me at the county office in Sanson to go and sit for my licence. I had no problems getting it.

Ngaire thinks she learnt about the WAAC from the newspaper.

They were wanting women to join up. I might have joined the Army anyway, because Dad had been in the Army in the First World War. He went overseas to the Middle East, after Gallipoli. He joined up and then, being on a farm, he was held back for 12 months before they'd let him go into camp. He was in camp down at Featherston. He and Mother were engaged before he went away, and he was

Previous page: *WAAC drivers from the Vehicle Reception Depot.* ATL, Gordon Burt Collection, F-15415-1/1
Above: *Ngaire Lawrence.* Ngaire Gibbons collection

away for, it must have been about four years, I suppose. He'd been back about 12 months before they got married. He was in a mounted rifles unit.

Did he talk about it?

No, not very much at all. None of them did. He left his appendix in Palestine. There must have been an Army hospital there. His older brother was over in the Middle East too. He was with the crowd who used to bring up supplies to the frontline on donkeys. I think they used to have a bit of fun with the donkeys.

WAACs about to begin a parade. ATL, Evening Post Collection, G–123865-1/2

What did you have to do to enlist?

I went to the Army recruiting office in King Street in Palmerston North. I had forms to fill in. At that stage I was under 21, so I had to take them home and get my parents' consent. I suppose it was only about six weeks after signing up that I got a letter to say that I had to report on a certain date down at the Miramar WAAC camp.

At home Ngaire cared for her mother, who was an invalid as a result of a brain haemorrhage.

How did your parents feel about you joining up?

They didn't mind, they understood. I could see that, being on a farm, I was going to be stuck in the land army, so that's why I got out first. Some of those girls who were in the land army had a pretty torrid time, by all accounts.

The family employed another young woman to take care of Ngaire's mother.

Tell me about your fiancé, Jim Gibbons, because you were engaged, weren't you?

Yes. I'd signed all my Army papers, but I hadn't sent them in when we got word that Jim was missing. That was the final bit that made me sign on the dotted line. My future father-in-law had a big radio and he was able to listen in to the Vatican, and they used to give out a list of names of those who'd been taken prisoner. About six weeks after I signed, we heard that Jim was all right and that he was a prisoner. He was in camp in Italy, and then the Italians threw in the sponge. I remember him saying that Italian guards locked their barracks one night and it was the Germans who unlocked them the next morning. They were put straight into cattle trucks and went up through the Brenner Pass into Germany, first to Stalag 8B [at Lamsdorf]. He was in 25 Battalion. He was captured at Ruweisat Ridge in the desert in 1942.

WAACs inside their hut. ATL, G-19080-1/4

In October 1942, Ngaire was told to report to camp at Miramar in Wellington.

We were given a voucher for the train fare. I got on the train at Feilding and there was a girl I'd been at school with. She spotted me getting on the train, so that was good, because there was somebody I knew right from the start. I remember one girl getting on at Levin wearing a fur coat.

We were met by an Army truck and driver, we piled into the back and drove out to Miramar. We were housed in wooden huts. They were made to take four bunks, but they only had three because in the other area they put wardrobes for us to hang our stuff in. We were the first crowd in there and were meant to be camp staff. I didn't want to be stuck as camp staff, I wanted a driving job. We were put into platoons for square-bashing, and I was such a pest to the sergeant in charge of our lot that about a week later when some girls came down from New Plymouth, who'd been sent down to be transport drivers, they got rid of me. There were supposed to be four girls but there were only three, so they poked me in as a fourth and that's how I came to get into the VRD, Vehicle Reception Depot.

We were a happy bunch there. There were about 8 of us for a while, but in the end there were about 20 in the unit. Our job was clearing the assembly lines. There was General Motors out at the Hutt, and the Ford Motor Company on Seaview Road, and New Zealand Motor Body Builders in Petone. There was another motor body builders in Ebor Street in Wellington. We used to take the cabs and chassis to the body builders. There were some that were just open chassis, so we put a couple of boards across and a fruit box on top, which we sat on. They were 15-hundredweight, small trucks. We drove those, right up to lumbering 11-ton AEC diesels. When the body builders were done, we would collect them and take them back to our unit, where they were officially marched in and given an NZ number, which was painted on the bonnet. There were two signwriters who used to do that job.

Ngaire was issued with her uniform the day after she arrived at Miramar.

We were taken up to the Winter Show building — they had a clothing store there — and we got smocks and lisle stockings and brown shoes, men's greatcoats to start with. It wasn't till later that they made the dress uniforms — the 'glamour suit'. I was one of the lucky ones, mine was made out of officers' material and there weren't a lot of us who got those. Later on they were a much rougher serge. Later we were issued with battledress that we wore while driving. It was more convenient climbing in and out of trucks.

How did you keep the trousers up?
A good question. I remember two or three of us went into Army Headquarters for some reason or other. We were wearing battledress and we must have walked past the store where they kept all the stuff, because I remember one of the guys stopping us and saying to us, 'Do you girls mind if we ask an impertinent question?' We said no. 'How do you keep your trousers up?' So we lifted our blouses and they could see we had them tied up with string. He roared with laughter and he said, 'Come on in here.' We went in and he issued us all with a pair of braces to hold our battledress trousers up, which was very good of him.

WAACs marching between huts, possibly at Miramar WAAC camp. ATL, G-19081-1/4

The training at Miramar was not too arduous.

It'd be about an hour in the morning, I suppose, and then the other girls were allocated jobs around the camp. There were those who had to do guard duty, there were those who were in the cookhouse, and those who did clerical work.

Were there women officers there at that stage?
There were one or two. The head of the camp, I think she was a lieutenant-colonel, and I think there was a captain. But many of those who were doing office work seemed to have commissions.

And how did you find army life — the discipline?
I quite enjoyed it. It never worried me because I'd been used to it at boarding school. Some of the other girls hadn't had that sort of experience, and they found it a bit tough.

What were the ablution blocks like?
They were just concrete floors with duckboards. They were chilly in the winter, but we survived. We had hot showers.

Did you have ID tags?
Yes, two. One was green. It had your name and your number on. The other one, I think it was a fawny colour, also had your name and your number. If you were killed, one was buried with you and one went back to the unit. All WAAC numbers started with '81'; '6' was the area we came from. The

General Motors Company, Petone.
ATL, Gordon Burt Collection, F-15616-1/1

Palmerston North/Wanganui area was Area 6; I must have been the 192nd in Area 6 to sign up so my number was 816192.

When you first started as a driver, did they give you tests to make sure you could drive those trucks?
We had our normal licence and we had our heavy traffic licence, so that said we could drive. The later ones who came into the unit, we early ones had to take them out and check them out.

> **The drivers in the Vehicle Reception Depot reported to Army Headquarters in Wellington each morning.**

We had to have our breakfast ahead of the main lot to get our tram into Army Headquarters in town. That took about three-quarters of an hour, I suppose. In the end they let us have a truck because we used to work late at night after the trams had stopped. I ended up taking the truck back to camp. The next morning, I'd set off in it and start picking up the others who lived at home and take them into town.

We had a 15-hundredweight truck, and on its front mudguard was A99. We'd pile into the back and go out to the factories in that. Our NCO would drive. We all had our own 'D' plates — demonstration plates, licence plates — and we had to tie those on, back and front.

We'd wander along, put our plates on, get in our trucks and wait till we were let out. The gatekeeper would have all the details of the trucks that we were taking away and would mark them off as we took them away.

How many times a day would you do that?

Twice a day — a trip in the morning, a trip in the afternoon. It depended a little bit on how many vehicles were coming off the assembly line. We liked it when they were turning out the jeeps. We used to race them along the Hutt Road. Oh boy, we used to have some fun in them! They could go, all right. We never got caught, because we were careful. One of our girls was going out with one of the Army traffic control guys, so he used to let us know [if we needed to be careful]. He particularly let us know where the one we called The Rat — the one who was out to catch us — was patrolling. We were very cautious in his area. He never caught any of us.

Bren carriers at Trentham military camp.
ATL, F-58041-1/2

After taking the truck chassis to the motor body builders, the WAAC drivers would take the finished trucks to a truck depot.

There were some we used to take out to the railway workshops where they put armoured bodies on them. I think they used to have Bren guns in them.

Ngaire vividly recalls driving Bren carriers to Trentham army camp. The WAAC moved 500 of them from General Motors.

They could be hairy to drive. They had tracks and the steering wheel was straight up and down. The damn things used to lock. They could be fun all right. We were taking them to Trentham, and I turned off the road to go down the little street into the Trentham gate, and the damn thing locked. I was going round and round. It took me a while to get it unlocked again. I had to stand up to unlock it. Some Army guy from the camp had seen me and reported me — something about showing off. I explained to our

A crowd at the races at Trentham during the war. Note the US flag. ATL, John Pascoe Collection, F-212-1/4

powers that be that I wasn't showing off. I said, 'The damned thing locked on me.' They understood immediately what I was talking about. Anyway, nothing came of that.

We were told to remember we were on duty 24 hours a day, seven days a week. All the stuff that went over to the Islands for the Third Division and T–Force and N–Force — that was Tonga and Norfolk Island — we had to assemble the vehicles to go to those places and take them down to the wharf to be loaded onto the ships. If there was a drizzle of rain the wharfies wouldn't work, so we'd have to take them back again and have another go the next night. That was over and above clearing the factories. We were kept busy.

Originally the truck depot the WAACs used was in part of the railway yards on Thorndon Quay.

God, what a filthy place that was, what with dust, dirt and of course the train smuts. We used to be filthy.

Eventually that depot was too small and so another Army vehicle parking area was set up in Porirua.

We had vehicles parked out at Porirua and there was a piece in *Truth* [newspaper] about all these Army vehicles exposed to the elements, so we had to shift them all. That's when we took them to Tauherenikau and parked them at the racecourse. They had a staff of mechanics and whatnot who lived under the grandstand at Tauherenikau and looked after them. There had to be mechanics to keep them in good order and run the motors every day or two, that sort of thing.

Ngaire did not mind driving the trucks over the Rimutaka Hill to Tauherenikau.

It didn't worry us, because we were bigger than the other vehicles on the road. When Trentham races were on, there'd be quite a bit of traffic coming over from the Wairarapa. People would save their petrol up to go to the races.

The WAAC drivers had a competition to see who could make the fastest trip over the hill.

The speed limit for Army vehicles was 30 miles an hour, so you had to be a little bit careful, but we managed to get up to about 40, which was really quite fast for those vehicles.

Was the road sealed?
No, I don't think it was. Most of the roads we went on weren't sealed. They were only sealed through townships and villages, and apart from that they were all metal.

It got to the stage that our parks were full and couldn't hold any more vehicles, so we had to get rid of the lot to make room for the others that were coming off the assembly lines. That's how we came to take them up to Waiouru. I think we used to do two trips a week. We'd be in a convoy of up to about 20 vehicles. The first Waiouru convoy was February 1944. Monday, a convoy of trucks to Waiouru; Tuesday, back to Wellington. Wednesday, clear the factories — they were slowing down — and Thursday, to Waiouru. Friday, back to Wellington. We did this for about eight months.

Ngaire recalls marching in parades through Wellington during the war.

We used to start at Kent Terrace, Cambridge Terrace, that area, then go through Wellington, down Lambton Quay towards the railway station. We were dismissed down there. There used to be a saluting base, and there'd be perhaps the Governor-General, or someone like that, on it. You'd march past and get, 'Eyes right! Eyes front!'

The WAACS wore their 'glamour suits' to march.

That used to annoy us because we would have much preferred to have marched in our battledresses, because that's what we normally wore.

After a short time at Miramar WAAC camp, Ngaire was shifted to the Dixon Street flats in central Wellington.

They were building them at that time and the Army took over a floor to house the WAACS, those of us who were working at Army Headquarters and CMD, Central Military District. They were quite nice flats. They put three girls in each one, and we had a shower and handbasin. I think there was a stove, because on weekends we could heat up food.

If you didn't do that, where would you go to eat when you were living there?
The YWCA in Boulcott Street. That food was nothing to preach about. We used to have a chit, and at lunchtime we could go to the restaurant at the railway station in Wellington — those of us who were out on the road. Later on we shifted from the Dixon Street flats to flats out at Woburn. They're not there any more.

The Dixon Street and Woburn flats were state housing built by the government.

They were partitioned off so that there were two girls to a room. Some of the partitions were halfway across windows and that sort of thing.

In 1944, Ngaire drove to Auckland in a convoy of six 6 x 6 GMC trucks. They were sealed and the drivers did not know what they were transporting.

There was a male officer who travelled in a car with our major at the front, and a wrecker vehicle trailed behind. The GMCs were 11-tonners. That was the only time we had two drivers to a truck. We picked them up from Taranaki Street, from a technical sort of place. We didn't know what was in them.

Years later, when Ngaire was staying with an old Army friend, she found out that the trucks contained radar gear and were being sent to the Pacific.

How long did it take you to get to Auckland?
The first truck broke down going up Ngauranga Gorge. We were supposed to be at Palmerston North showgrounds — that was an Army camp during the war — for lunch. We didn't get there till about two o'clock. We had lunch, and we had to hang around till they'd fixed the truck. Then we went to Waiouru. It was about six o'clock when we left Palmerston, so we had quite a night of it. We stayed in the hospital, in a ward, because there were no other WAACs at Waiouru.

Where did you go from there?
To Hamilton. There was no Desert Road then, so we had to come back and go round up through Taumarunui.

On the third day, they reached Auckland.

We had them on the dock half an hour ahead of schedule. We were very proud of ourselves.

Was there ever any chance of you going overseas?

I applied to go, but Mother became ill and I had to say no. It would have been to the Middle East, but some of the WAACs were being sent from there to England to man clubs, knowing that the ex-POWs would all be coming out through England. That was why I wanted to get there.

In October 1944, the Vehicle Reception Depot was disbanded because by then few trucks were being produced at the factories.

Members of the Vehicle Reception Depot. ATL, Gordon Burt Collection, F-117807-1/2

Where did you go then?

I went to Army Headquarters, the transport office. I was bored stiff. There were blessed great petrol things that had to be filled in. Sheets about 45 centimetres square. Petrol's the most awful stuff to keep track of. I wasn't there very long really, as that's when Mother became ill and I had to go home. I was on leave without pay.

Ngaire recalls hearing that the war in Europe had ended in May 1945.

I was at home. I can remember feeling a bit annoyed because I couldn't leave Mother, so I couldn't get into town and join in any of the festivities. People knew the Allies were winning, there was no doubt about that.

Did you hear much about how the war was going overseas?

We used to listen to the radio. I suppose the news we got was censored. We only got the general idea of how things were going — Battle of Britain and that sort of thing. I think most people understood that it wasn't actually the Germans, it was Hitler that was the problem.

Did you have any personal feelings about them because of your fiancé being taken prisoner?

No, not really, because after he came home he said that they'd been treated very well. He much preferred the Germans to the Italians. He said the Germans were more dependable.

> **In 1945, Jim Gibbons was in a POW camp in German Silesia, now part of Poland. Along
> with other POWs he was marched by the Germans from the camp into Czechoslovakia,
> where he was liberated by US troops. He was sent to England to recuperate and returned to
> New Zealand on the Orion. Ngaire had been discharged from the Army in July 1945, and the
> couple married in 1946. Using a rehabilitation loan, they bought a farm at Tangimoana from
> Jim's uncle. They had three daughters, Robyn, Margaret and Suzanne. Jim died aged 33.**

Robyn wasn't quite four. She's the only one who's got a very vague memory of her father. The others don't remember him at all.

Jim Gibbons.
Ngaire Gibbons collection

What was it like for you, having to farm and bring up little girls by yourself?
It didn't give me time to worry about myself. I employed single labour and built a bach where the worker lived. He would have his meals in the house. I had some awfully nice guys working on the place over the years.

> *Ngaire attends Anzac Day services at Rongotea each year, and also meets up with other ex-WAACs in Palmerston North at the RSA once a month. She is a member of the Ex-WAACs Association and attended WAAC reunions after the war.*

What would you do at those?
Talk mostly. A concert might be put on, or something like that.

> *She reflects on her wartime service as a driver.*

I thoroughly enjoyed my time in the Army. I made good friends, got companionship. It's certainly an experience I'm very pleased I had.

'WE TRAINED ON THE PREDICTORS'

Hazel ROWE, W820296, Sergeant, WAAC

Hazel Davis, one of the three children of Leonard and Bessie Davis, was born in Christchurch in 1923. Hazel's brother Lindsay served in the Merchant Navy on the Pamir *during the Second World War, and her sister Norma was a nurse at Christchurch Hospital. Leonard Davis had served in the Navy during the First World War, although he saw no action as he did not enlist till near the end. During the Second World War, Leonard was in the National Reserve initially, and was then seconded to the Air Force because of his expertise as a telegraphist. Although he was in his early forties, he went to the Solomon Islands. Hazel worked at Hay's department store when she left school. Hazel's mother's house became a base for Hazel's Army friends when they were on leave in Christchurch.*

WHEN THE WWSA CAME ALONG, I used to go to that once a week. We studied transport and signalling, and did drill on a Saturday out in Hagley Park, shouting orders across the park.

What appealed to you about the WWSA?

We did signalling, and mechanics taught us about car engines. At one time they wanted a group to go and pick tomatoes at Heathcote, so we went to pick tomatoes and got 10 shillings. They took ninepence off us for tax. We had a drum section and used to play in front of marches, in parades. We used to go to the garages on a Saturday. They'd make a fault on a car engine, and you had to find that fault and repair it. They'd take all the leads off the distributor. You were taught how to disable it so no one could steal it. You had to learn how to put all those leads back on your distributor, and change tyres.

We had a khaki uniform, quite creamy khaki with a peak cap. WWSA was just one night a week,

Previous page: *WAACs at Mt Pleasant battery, near Lyttelton.* Hazel Rowe collection
Above: *Hazel Davis.* Hazel Rowe collection
Opposite: *Hazel Davis in her WWSA uniform.* Hazel Rowe collection

or perhaps a Saturday. I suppose there'd be, thinking back now, no more than 50 or 60 of us. It was mostly signals, and I think they had first aid as well. It depended what you wanted to do. I think I chose the signals because of my father's background.

What made you choose the Army?

I don't know. I suppose it was a carry on from the WWSA. There must have been an advertisement to make me interested. A lot of WAACs went out to Godley Head, and I thought, I'll be going out to Godley Head, but I didn't get out there. Some did. They were working in heavy anti-aircraft, naval guns, really. You just went in. You didn't know what you were going to do because we were spread around in all kinds of jobs.

Hazel recalls the enlistment process in the WAAC in August 1942.

You had to apply and you got a form to fill in. You had to have it signed by your parents, and get two references. I got one from Mr Hay and one from my church minister — I've still got them after all these years. Then you went down to the King Edward Barracks, where you had to have a medical. They checked out your eyes, your heart, nothing much. We were all pretty fit in those days. We didn't have cars, we walked everywhere.

Then I joined the Army and went out to Addington racecourse. I always laugh, because I was only in three weeks and I got three stripes. I'd done all the other training, so I knew the drill. I got 30 girls and had to teach them their left foot from their right. I used to take them round behind the huts at night, one or two of them, and teach them how to march.

Hazel Davis (front left) leads her platoon at Addington racecourse, Christchurch 1942. They are wearing men's battledress. Hazel Rowe collection

I was there for three months. I was a drill sergeant, what was called a 'corporal, acting sergeant'. I got paid a corporal's pay but I had to do a sergeant's job. There were no privileges as far as a sergeants' mess or anything like that. You were just one of the girls.

My job was to train them all in marching, and we had a lot of lectures on folding blankets. We had guard duty on the gate. There was so many on each night. When they had a route march, you had to inspect their feet when they came back to see they didn't have blisters. We were issued with men's battledress, boots, heavy socks and a big greatcoat, because they didn't have any uniforms for the girls. They hadn't prepared. The North Island had them but the South Island didn't. We had men's battledress with brass buttons, and flies. We never had skirts. It was a long time until we got dress uniforms. We got smocks issued. They were dresses, buttoned down the front, in a light khaki colour.

Eventually we got the female battledress, with the same top, but no brass buttons. We got socks, boots and gaiters. I suppose they were to keep your trousers tidy. Everyone wore them. We had caps when we first went in, felt caps, then in 1943 we got berets. Berets were good. You didn't wear them inside the building, but if you went out you had to have your hat on.

I had to check up each night to see that everybody was in camp. Addington was a racecourse. They had rows of huts. You had the grandstand and then you had a concrete space and the huts were on the grass place right beside it. There were two camps, the men's and the women's. Our ablution blocks were the public blocks that the public used on race days, and you had to go way across in the morning or night or cold weather, whenever it was, right across there if you wanted to go to the ablution blocks or the showers.

The officers who were training you, were they men?
They were men, sergeants, and we had Mrs Kerr, our officer. She had three pips, I think — she'd be a subaltern or captain.

Can you remember the first day there?
We went down to King Edward Barracks and were all loaded into the back of an Army truck and off we went. We arrived at the racecourse and got our hut and blankets and so forth. They were very small two-man huts. Wooden slats on the bunk, good for the backbone. We had to go and get straw and stuff our own mattresses.

It was basic training right from the start. We all lined up by our huts in our platoons, and marched across to the main grandstand. Underneath the grandstand was the mess room. There were only about three or four men there, drill sergeants and a couple of officers. The men's camp was a different part altogether. We had nothing to do with them — not that I know of!

We learnt to salute: longest way up, shortest way down. We had to salute all the officers when we saw them. We had a lot of drill, day after day after day, to get everyone organised into open march, close ranks, left turn, right turn, right dress, and all this type of thing. People had to learn how to march properly and swing their arms properly. There were a few that were very, very difficult to teach, but still they came round. It was only basic training.

Did any of the girls decide they wanted to go home?
No. They couldn't go home. Most of them were volunteers, so it was their choice.

There was a rec room there. We got together, sat around, talked to one another. There wasn't much doing at all. By the time they'd worked us all day, it was time to go to bed. There was a piano. We'd have a sing-song, but there wasn't a great deal of getting together at Addington that I can remember.

We all got our injections there too, for tetanus and typhoid. We got 24 hours off duty when we got those. We were going in for breakfast and we could see them with the needles. They lined you all up and you went in a long line — bang, bang, bang, bang. You had a sore arm for a while, too.

All the WAACs at Addington were from the South Island.

Some went back to Dunedin, down to Taiaroa Heads. Some went to offices in Timaru. There were offices in Christchurch too — the optician's office, and headquarters. There was an artillery battery at Nelson. Some went down to Godley Head, some went to Battery Point, so they were spread out.

Hazel remembers how people who committed offences were punished.

They got pay docked, mostly. I had to march a few in occasionally. They had an escort either side.

What sorts of things would they do?
People might be two or three days late coming back off leave. We didn't have much in the way of that, though. We docked their pay a couple of days, or something like that.

How did you deal with the discipline?
It didn't worry me. It was nothing out of the ordinary, just common sense.

At the end of 1942, Hazel was sent to Trentham camp near Wellington for officer training, but was then told she could not go because she was not 21. However, the Army changed its mind again and let her attend the course.

We knew we were only going to fill the numbers. We learnt military law, we were treated the same as the male officers. We did cross-country marching, cross-country night map-reading, shooting with Bren guns, .303, Vickers, pistol.

After six weeks' training, Hazel went home to Christchurch on leave before returning to Wellington to train at the School of Artillery in Melrose in January 1943.

School of Artillery, formerly the Truby King Karitane Hospital, Melrose, Wellington.
ATL, F-438-1/4

We trained on the predictors with the anti-aircraft guns. There's what they call a TOC–I instrument, and that was a small telescope type of thing, about three feet long. That spied the plane that was coming over — the enemy plane. Then you had the rangefinder, which could be six, seven feet long, with a camera at each end. You looked into that and that brought down the range of the plane. The predictor was connected to the rangefinder and had six little dials all round, and that followed the instruments. You had to keep your pointer lined up all the time, and that traced the plane, following the height, the speed, and where it would be in such and such a time. The predictor was joined up to the guns by coaxial cables.

The dials turned gearing inside the predictor to calculate the range (from the change in angle and estimated speed) and direction of motion. The information from the predictor drove motors attached to the traversing and elevating gears of the gun.

Hazel Davis (left) with WAACs and a predictor at 83 Heavy Anti-Aircraft Battery, Mt Pleasant, near Lyttelton.
Hazel Rowe collection

The predictors were lined up on the guns, and the guns were very dependent on them. You had two men, one on either side of the gun, with handles for elevation. The women did all the instrument work that the guns depended on.

The shells had a fuse cap. The fuse was set to what the predictor was telling that gun. They put the shell in and the fuse cap was twisted round to the time. When it left the gun, the predictor had worked out where the plane was going to be when the shell got there. The fuse cap was a brass cover on the end of the shell, about three inches long and shaped like a cone. That came off and they turned the point of the shell onto a certain fuse setting, for so many seconds. The shells were at least two feet long. Three point seven inches round the base. They were heavy.

Was it hard to learn how to do it?
You had to concentrate.

Hazel Davis has her smoko in a wheelbarrow while making brick paths at Mt Pleasant. Hazel Rowe collection

Tell me about when you went home on leave from Trentham on the Wahine.

We got leave, starting 18th December. I got the train in from Trentham to Wellington, and went on board the *Wahine*. There were, I think, 600 male soldiers going home on leave and 30 girls. We got cabins. We got out into the harbour at about eight o'clock and bang! We hit the *South Sea* right in the middle of Wellington harbour, amidships. It was a minesweeper. The *Wahine* would have had the right of way because it's a mail boat. If the minesweeper had been sweeping it would have had the right of way, but it wasn't. It took a while to sink because they had to let the steam out. The siren was going the whole time, which brought everybody down to the harbour. There was nobody hurt and nobody lost.

We stayed on board. There was a bit of damage to the front of the *Wahine*. They took us back to the wharf and inspected what had happened, but off we went.

> *After training at the School of Artillery, Hazel went on furlough and then was posted to 83 Heavy Anti-Aircraft Battery at Mt Pleasant, near Lyttelton, in early February 1943. At the same time she was promoted to sergeant.*

The Battery was right up on the Port Hills above Lyttelton; we could look from the gun park down to Lyttelton, and from the accommodation huts down to Sumner.

They had four 3.7 guns, a mess hall, and a small canteen — one girl ran the small canteen. The shop opened up every now and then. We had a nurse on duty, an orderly room, offices, a telephone exchange, and mess duties. There were about 80 girls there. There was a medical inspection room. One of the WAACs was a VAD, and you saw her if you had any illnesses or anything. We had a recreation hut and we could meet at night and have music if we wanted. People came up from Godley Head, from Battery Point, and down in Mt Pleasant, where there was a signals section. We'd have dances.

We stayed in four-man huts. I suppose they'd be about twelve feet by eight. No lights, no lining; it was cold in the winter. We went up there in the summer and got snow later on. It's a funny thing, but no one complained. You just went along with it.

There was a big fire down in Lyttelton, and some building got burnt down. It was a brick building, so they salvaged all the bricks, brought them all up and we had to make paths. We laid bricks and made paths between all the huts and round about, but were no sooner finished than along came the Public Works and scooped them all up and put concrete down.

We had live shoots. You practised and practised for days and days and weeks on end, with a Harvard zooming over the top of the trig station. On a live shoot, you'd have a Tiger Moth towing this great big drogue about 20 feet long. They used to shoot out over the sea, over Sumner. Loud! You can imagine four guns shooting over you. No headphones. Tin hats. We used to wear our tin hats in the wet weather to keep the rain off.

There were a lot of men — the ones who were loading the guns, and transport drivers. Girls were transport drivers too. There was one woman officer. For a while we had Kit Catto and then Ursula Gunn. The girls would work much more willingly with an officer who could speak to them, as opposed to one who would just order them.

What do you think the WAAC officers were like, on the whole?
Mavis Davidson was very good. The two or three officers I'd been through OCTU with were OK, but I never worked with them. Most of them were all right. One or two were a bit uppish.

Out at the battery they had a sergeants' mess and there were three WAAC sergeants up there, I think, to start with. We used to have to dine with the sergeants in the sergeants' mess, but the food was

The gun park at 83 Heavy Anti-Aircraft Battery, Mt Pleasant, 1943. The cases at front right contain shells. Hazel Rowe collection

dreadful. The sergeants complained and said, 'Could we have the same as the gunners?' Once you went to a battery you weren't a private, you were a gunner. The girls were all gunners and bombardiers.

For a while I was the only WAAC sergeant in there with all those men, but, you know, they never put a foot wrong. They'd tell a story and say sorry, and I'd say, 'What?' It had gone over my head. If a lady behaves like a lady, a man will behave like a gentleman. I never had any problems at all. Some of the men were married men. I got the job of sewing the stripes on and doing buttons. We could have liquor in the sergeants' mess, but you had to pay your share whether you drank or not — not that we drank very much.

On the battery, when it was wet, we couldn't be on the command post because we were out in the open. We'd go into gun emplacements. Right round the edges there were big concrete cupboard things. The shells were stacked on shelves in there. We used to have to pull them out, put them on our shoulder, and wipe all the moisture off the shell. That was just filling in time, I reckon.

The command post and gun emplacements were located further up the hill, above the accommodation.

We marched up from where our huts were. It'd be about a quarter of a mile up to the top of the hill where the guns were. The command post was on a flat section — when I say 'flat', it was rocky and dreadful, but it was the flat part.

> *After around nine months with 83 Heavy Anti-Aircraft Battery at Mt Pleasant, Hazel was posted to Burnham camp near Christchurch, where she remained until after the end of the war.*

The girls were dispersed throughout the whole camp. A lot of them were in ordnance, that's supplies, and there were girls in transport, girls in the exchange, camp headquarters, as dental assistants. You had them as nurses, VADS, you had them in all the messes throughout the camp. They took over everything the men were doing so the men were free to go overseas.

What did you actually do?
I was in WAAC headquarters, with the records. That was in E Block itself, not the camp headquarters. We had a map of the whole block so we knew where every girl was sleeping, what duties they were on, when they were on leave, when they were not on leave. I wrote out their leave passes when they went out, collected them when they came back and marked them off. We had a big recreation hall attached to E Block. They could go in there at night and sing, or do what they liked. All those wartime songs — 'White Cliffs of Dover', 'Roll Out the Barrel'. We had a swimming pool at Burnham and the girls could go down at certain hours, but they always had to have a sergeant there in case any of the men came round.

Did any of the girls get pregnant?
We had one girl, but she was engaged to the chap. Another girl got pregnant and went out and had the baby. Another girl came in from another camp after having had a child. When you take 300 girls, you only had a case of three; for 300 girls that's not bad.

They weren't discharged?
They'd be transferred to another camp. After all, they're human.

Did you get quite regular leave while you were there?

You could go out and back on a Friday night, or you could go out on a weekend. You'd go out Saturday midday and come back Sunday, by train. It was 18 miles from Burnham to Christchurch. The men were in the front and you had to make sure that the windows were all intact when you went and when you came back, and that no men came through. The train seats faced one way going, and faced another way coming back. Sometimes some of the girls didn't have tickets, so they'd put the seats so that one went one way and one the other way, hang a greatcoat over them and sneak in underneath.

Hazel recalls what happened at Burnham before a reinforcement of men was sent overseas.

They spiked the railway lines. You couldn't ring out. It was a secret, you see. We were all warned — you took all your washing off the line, otherwise you found bras and knickers up the flagpoles. They did all kinds of naughty things, those men, then off they went in the early hours of the morning.

Did you ever get the opportunity to go overseas?

No, you had to be 21. I didn't want to go anyway. I could have gone. Some went up to the Islands, some went to the Middle East. After the war quite a few went up to Jayforce.

At the end of the war, a number of British servicemen who had been in Changi prison camp came to Burnham.

We got friendly with a few of them. Some of those boys hadn't heard from home, some found their wives had married again. One had had his appendix out without anaesthetic. I took one home on leave, and next thing I knew there were three girls walking up the drive with three more of them. Dad had come back from overseas then, and they all got on together. One guy came to the door and wouldn't come in. He hadn't been in a house for eight years. He'd been in the permanent army, gone out to India, then got taken. It was a funny thing. Mum had cooked rhubarb, and the last thing he'd eaten before he'd left England, eight years before, was rhubarb. They settled in and were there about six or eight weeks, and off they went home again on the *Monowai* hospital ship.

New Zealand airmen who looked after freed Allied prisoners of war. ATL, C.L. Campbell Collection, F-111668-1/2

What was their health like?
They weren't too bad. They'd been taken out of Changi and had been on the hospital ship or in hospital and they had been fed up, as it were.

What about mentally?
Some weren't the best, no.

Tell me about getting out of the Army.
If you were going to get married, you applied for your discharge. I got out in December 1945 and got married on 12 January. You applied to get out, and signed a paper. The officer had to sign it, then you

went into town and got your discharge paper. After you left you had to take your uniform back. You got £25 when you returned your Army uniform. You could keep your boots though. They were good for gardening.

How did you meet your husband?

At a dance. My aunty used to have a social club, a church thing. The men from Wigram would come and dance with the girls. Ted Rowe was in the Air Force, from Auckland. We met and went out together, and corresponded while he was overseas. He proposed to me while he was overseas. He was in Grimsby, then St Anne's-on-Sea, and then South Shields, erecting high towers for radar. Then he went to Burma and was attached to the Royal Air Force out there, on radar, with the Chindits raiders. They were cut off by the Japs and went through a few things that weren't very nice. They flew them out in the end with what they stood up in. The first we knew was when his mother wrote to me and said she'd heard he was near New Zealand. He was away about four years. He must have got home in 1945. He was in the Air Force for quite a while in Wellington before he got out.

Ted Rowe took an adult apprenticeship as an electrician after war. The couple married in Christchurch and moved to Auckland. Hazel worked for a real estate agent until her oldest son, Ian, was born. The couple had two more sons, Lloyd and Peter. Hazel, now a widow, still lives in Auckland.

Do you think the war changed you?

I think it makes you stronger. You had to get on — I'd never left home before. It didn't worry me because I was with others. In Burnham I knew all the girls. I went home on leave. You had discipline and regular hours: up at six, lights out at ten. And look out if you weren't in bed!

'THEY WERE CALLING FOR VOLUNTEERS'

Katherine DYALL, W813320, Gunner, WAAC

Kath Martin, Ngati Maniapoto, Ngati Paoa and Tamatera, was born in Otorohanga in February 1923. Her father, Walter Martin, was a taxi driver, but he died when Kath and her two sisters were young. Her mother was born Miriam Paeriakina Hughes. When Kath left school, aged 14, she worked as a shop assistant in Otorohanga.

What happened that made you decide to join the Army?

I got sick of working in the fruit shop and I said to my friends, 'I'm going to join the Army.' They said, 'You wouldn't pass. You're too short.' I said, 'I'll soon prove to you', so I put in my application. I had to go to Hamilton for my medical, and they were all at the station when the train pulled up. I was yelling out, 'I've passed!' Well, they all joined up after me. Most of them went to the Air Force, because they had a station in Te Awamutu, and most of them went there. I think I was the only one that went into the Army. My girlfriend couldn't get in because she had poor eyesight.

Before I went into the Army, the train used to go through and pick up men who'd volunteered — because Maoris weren't conscripted, they were volunteers. We would go up to the station with the ones going from Otorohanga and see all these people going to camp. They had to go to Papakura, and I didn't realise that I would soon be doing the same thing.

Did you have to be 18 before you could join?

Yes.

Tell me about the medical — what did they do?

Well, they examined your [private parts] and your chest.

Previous page: *WAACs on parade at Fort Dorset, Wellington.* ATL, W.H. Raine Collection, G-20868-1/4
Above: *Kath Martin.* Katherine Dyall collection

Otorohanga railway station. ATL, A.P. Godber Collection, G-815-1/2-APG

It was a male doctor.

It was very embarrassing, but you had to do it. I mean, I was so innocent, because my mother never discussed anything. We didn't know about sex.

What made you choose the Army?
Because that's where they were calling for volunteers.

What did your mother think?
Actually, she didn't seem to mind. It was my grandmother. When I got called up to report to camp, my grandmother took sick. She thought I was going overseas, I think. It was terrible to leave her sick, because we had to go to Papakura and train for six weeks. In six weeks I got leave and went home. She was so pleased to see me. I didn't have a uniform. She asked me in Maori, 'Where's your clothes?' I said

WAACs unload pillows from a truck. ATL, PAColl-8846

that I hadn't been issued with a uniform. My granny couldn't speak English. My mother spoke both, mostly in English. I'd answer them in Maori.

Kath — who was known as 'Midge' in the Army because of her lack of height — thinks it was about three or four weeks after she passed her medical that she went to Papakura for training.

They were setting up [anti-aircraft] batteries because the Japanese had entered into the war. A lot of men who were in the batteries were called up to go overseas, and that's how the women got to take over some of the men's jobs. The girls went on the searchlights; some went into signals. I don't think they ever had anything to do with firing the guns.

Did they tell you what you had to take with you to camp?
We had to take our civilian clothes and pocket money, and that was it. When we got there we got issued with our things. We had to fill up our own palliasse with straw to sleep on. By the time I got

there, I had enough stuff in my hands that I didn't fill up my palliasse properly. I had so much stuff to carry around. Well, I suffered, because half the time the hay would go down to the bottom and I slept on the boards. Luckily it was only for six weeks.

Was there anybody else that you knew?
Yes, one girl who came from Te Kuiti. She was married and she had two children. She joined because her husband was overseas in the Maori Battalion and it was one of her wishes to go over there.

When Kath arrived at Papakura Camp, there were Army trucks waiting at the station.

There were men too, not only us girls — the whole train was full of volunteers going into camp.

How did the men treat you when you got on the train?
They treated us all right. They were young too, like us. I think they all were nervous, just like us — wondering what was going to happen.

The training was mostly learning how to march and how to salute and how to obey orders. They told you to do what they wanted and not what you wanted to do.

Did you find that hard?
Not really, because my mother was really strict; well, not really strict, but you knew that you were only allowed to do certain things.

What about living together, how did you find that?
It didn't worry me. We were the second lot of girls to go in, and the showers were still set up how the men had their showers, with no screen or anything. It was very embarrassing when you were not used to changing in front of other people. But it was different when we got to Castor Bay, because the girls had their own toilets and showers.

How long was it before you got your uniform?
I can't remember. Our first issue was the field cap and greatcoat. Then, after a while, we got issued with

shoes, and then with our stockings. You looked so ridiculous — field cap and coat, khaki stockings and shoes, and our own dress.

Then they gave us a smock. We had one smock for day wear, that we worked in around the camp, and one for going out. After that they issued us with a skirt and a tie. The smock was so big that a lot of girls made pleats at the back, which made it more feminine. We starched the collar with cornflour, and sometimes you'd overdo it and the collar would be like cardboard. But, in the end, I think the uniform became very smart. There were brass buttons down the jacket. You had to polish them every day. I was proud of it.

You had to have your hair an inch above your collar. You could have make-up, but make-up was hard to buy. There was not much jewellery. You could wear rings, but that was about it. Sleepers were allowed, but in those days not many women had their ears pierced.

Were you ever allowed to wear trousers?
Yes, we got issued with trousers in winter. Khaki trousers and boots. In the mess, you had to scrub the floor with caustic soda and they came in handy for doing jobs like that.

Kath Martin (front row, centre) with other WAACs at Castor Bay.
Katherine Dyall collection

When did you start work in the mess?
As soon as I got to Castor Bay. I didn't know where Castor Bay was. We went on Army trucks. They dropped us off, myself and a couple of guys, and the rest went to the islands, Motutapu and Motuihe. We had two girls who worked in the office, and one worked in Army issue. There were about six in the officers' mess. We didn't have a woman officer. I must have been in the Army about 18 months before we got Miss Jackson. I was her batwoman. She knew me

A dance for US troops in Wellington, 1943. Fran McGowan collection

from Papakura. I had to make her bed, lay out her uniform. She was very nice.

I think we were very good girls. We'd go down to the YMCA and we knew that at nine o'clock we had to be back in our own dormitory. There was no funny business. My boyfriend, my future husband, used to come and we'd walk back down together. No kiss kiss. He'd go up to his dormitory and I'd go up to mine.

Kath recalls the work in the officers' mess at Castor Bay.

We had our cook, and he'd give us the menu. It was just like waitressing. You'd take the menu to the

OC, officer commanding, and you always served him first. After that, they ordered what they wanted and you'd go back and tell the cook. They'd serve it and we'd take it in. That was about it. A couple would be on the dishes. Then we were finished.

In the mornings you had to set your bed up for inspection. You had to fold the blankets a certain way, put your shoes on a certain way. When the inspection was over, you had to make up your bed. We did that every day — they inspected the dormitories every morning. It was hard, because you had to have your blanket exactly right — the markings all in a row. We were lucky, the girls, because we got issued with sheets. The men didn't.

There were plenty of ways to spend spare time at Castor Bay. People from the Army Education Welfare Service took classes.

They had someone come and teach you how to dressmake, pattern drafting, embroidery and things like that. People volunteered to entertain you — singers or dancers. The camp put on concerts. We used to sing some of Vera Lynn's songs, and we used to make up our own. When we went on the Army trucks, we'd start singing.

Some played netball. It all depended on you. Some of them played tennis. There was always something to do. I did a bit of fancywork. I used to write to my mother, and when friends were overseas I used to write to them. At night time we'd go down to the YMCA and be entertained, or play table tennis.

There were dances at the town hall when the Americans arrived. They invited us WAACs to be partners at their welcome to Auckland, welcome to New Zealand. I danced at the Governor-General's residence in Auckland, and the girls went to Whangaparaoa because the Army was settled there. You had to stand up and dance because that's what you were there for, although some of them couldn't dance. We wore full uniform. A lot of the girls, you could tell they went out with Americans because they had American Camel cigarettes.

John Dyall. Katherine Dyall collection

Did they talk to you about sex education and venereal disease and things like that?
Yes, we did that in Papakura. It was the first time I'd ever heard of that. And when you came back from leave you got examined. They thought you might have been a naughty girl.

I got in the habit of smoking there, because everybody else was smoking. Some of the girls didn't even know how to roll a cigarette and they bought a machine, put their tobacco in and rolled it up, whereas my mother smoked and I'd watched her rolling a cigarette, so I knew how to do that.

When I turned 21 I wanted to go home, but they stopped all leave. I went up to the major and said, 'I want to go home. My mother's a widow. She's putting on my 21st birthday.' The major said no, so they celebrated my 21st birthday without me being there. Mum couldn't cancel it because she'd prepared all the food. One of my friends said it was so funny — awful — sitting there eating and I was not there.

> *Kath spent about 18 months at Castor Bay before being sent to North Head, where she worked in the general mess. She was then transferred to Hopuhopu (near Ngaruawahia) to await her discharge from the Army, which happened before the war ended.*

John, my future husband, was still in the Army. He was waiting to be discharged. I was back in Otorohanga.

> *Kath had met John Dyall when they were both posted to Castor Bay. When John was transferred to North Head, they wrote to each other every day. One of the girls in Kath's dorm, who also came from Otorohanga, was the colonel's chauffeur. She was a 'runner' and would deliver and collect Kath's and John's mail. John was based at Bastion Point when he was discharged from the Army. In 1946, the couple were married.*

I wore a blue costume, jacket and skirt, because everything was still rationed. When my husband and I got married, we got a rehab loan to build a house in Hamilton.

> *John Dyall had begun his accountancy studies in the Army and became a qualified accountant after the war. The couple had four children — two sons and two daughters — and lived in Hamilton, Gisborne and Porirua before settling in Wellington. Kath, now a widow, still lives in Wellington close to her whanau.*

GWEN STEVENS, W3492,
LEADING AIRCRAFTWOMAN, WAAF

Gwen Pollard was born in Auckland in 1921. Her father Herbert, who had established the timber firm Henderson & Pollard, and her mother Lucy lived with their large family of nine children in Mt Eden. Gwen left Epsom Girls' Grammar School at the end of the Fifth Form and went to work as a cashier in the hardware department of the Farmers' Trading Company. After her sister married, she worked at home as a companion to her mother. Gwen recalls hearing that war had been declared in September 1939.

I REMEMBER my father would listen to the radio at nine o'clock every night, and we all had to listen to that. I can remember 'This is the World News. BBC calling', then war was declared. Of course, it wasn't all that long since the Great War had finished, and my father's brother Norman was killed in that war. The first thing my brother Norman wanted to do was join up. My father wasn't very happy about it, but we were all patriotic, so he did join up.

In 1941, Gwen became engaged to Max Cronin.

Max joined the Air Force and went over to Canada, but before he went my father said yes, we could get engaged. He went to Canada, then to England and up to Scotland. He was flying Lancasters, and, I think, on the third flight out he was shot down over Düsseldorf, and he was killed.

I was out at Piha when my father came out on New Year's morning to tell me. He didn't tell me all day until he said, 'Gwen, I want to talk to you.' I thought, What have I done now? My shorts are too short, I've got too much lipstick on, or something — because I was always getting into trouble. Then he took me away to the bedroom and told me that Max was missing, believed killed.

Previous page: *Releasing a weather balloon outside Northern Group Headquarters, 1944.* RNZAF Official, via
Air Force Museum, Christchurch, PR3529
Above: *Gwen Pollard.* Gwen Stevens collection

Mt Eden Road, 1927, looking north towards Mt Eden.
Special Collections, Auckland City Libraries, 7-A10943

Right: *This photograph of the Rutland Street drill hall was taken in 1968, but it had changed little since the 1940s.* Special Collections, Auckland City Libraries 7-A13534

When I came back to Auckland, I said to him, 'I don't care what you say, Dad, but I'm going to join the Air Force.' And he said, 'I'm proud of you. Yes, you can do that', because I wasn't 21 and you couldn't join without your parents' permission till you were 21. You had to go in and apply, and then you took the papers home and your parents had to sign them, then you took them back in and they gave you a medical exam. This was quite early, there were not many women at all.

After gaining her parents' permission, Gwen had to have a medical examination at the Rutland Street drill hall.

You had to take all your clothes off, and I was horrified. I think we all went in together and he did a pretty quick examination. I was not brought up like that.

Then they sent us to Wellington. We had to go on a train, and I think it was very poorly arranged. There would have been 10 of us in the carriage, and they didn't put any of us together. They put a man with us, and to this day I can remember the man sitting beside me. Every time I'd start to go to sleep his hands would wander. He kept saying, 'Put your head on my shoulder, dear.' Today I would have pressed the button or called the guard, but I didn't know what to do. But I survived.

In Wellington, Gwen went to Air Headquarters and was sworn in after meeting the WAAF second-in-charge, Squadron Leader Elsie Carlyon. There was no room at the WAAF hostel — or Waafery — in Molesworth Street, so at first Gwen lived at the YWCA.

Three days after I got there, the Americans arrived. They hadn't seen a woman for six weeks. I was a very fast runner. You had to hop off the tram and run as fast as you could up this little street where the YWCA was. If the men could grab you they would, and push you into a doorway. I never got grabbed, I dodged.

Would they say things to you?
Oh yes, they'd make suggestions, but when you got to know them they were different, I think. Every Saturday night we would get taken by a truck up to the YWCA dance. You had to dance. A lot of the people there were American, but there were a lot of New Zealand forces, too. Sometimes they'd take us to Rongotai. The Americans brought one of their big bands out to Rongotai.

What did you wear to those dances?
We had to go in uniform.

The WAAF uniforms were not ready when Gwen enlisted.

They had to be tailored. They took three or four weeks to do that. In the meantime we were running around in ordinary civilian clothes. Then we got two skirts, a jacket, blue bloomers — I never wore

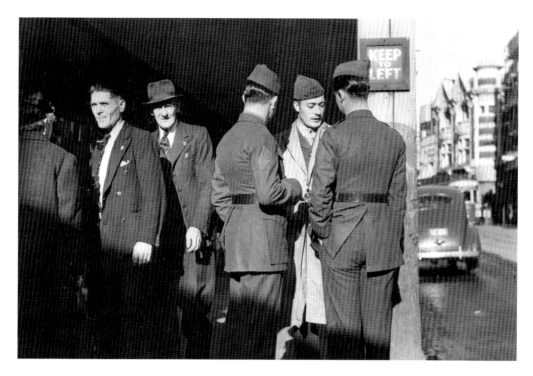

US Marines in Manners Street, Wellington, July 1943. ATL, War History Collection, F-503-1/4

those. We got lisle stockings, black shoes, two shirts, a cardigan, gloves and the beret. Eventually we got greatcoats, but that was quite a lot later. I was never in trousers, but if you were in the transport division, you were allowed to wear trousers. I was allowed to wear my engagement ring, but nothing much else, I think.

We did a bit of marching. When we went on duty we used to march from the Waafery down to the Air Headquarters, and I think we marched back when we came off duty at night, because we kept more or less office hours when at headquarters. If we went anywhere together, we'd have to march, smartly.

I was in the Signals Division and was what they called a 'runner'. The signals would come through and be printed out and they'd go to some other part of the building, or to one of two or three other buildings in that bottom part of Wellington. I'd have to take the signal to the office in some other part of the building, and then come back. One of the signals I had to take was the confirmation of my fiancé's death. It was pretty sad, and I think the matron was quite sorry for me. I know that I was very, very homesick, as you can imagine, being a spoilt little girl, and my parents were a bit worried about me so they sent my brother Carlton down to Wellington. I can remember he gave me £5. That was just so much money.

In 1942, there were two strong earthquakes in the Wellington region and Gwen experienced them both.

The first one was when we were in Molesworth Street, and I remember the whole room was rocking. The light was going backwards and forwards. In the toilet, which was next door to me, you could hear all the water sloshing. There was a big wall in the passageway which was full of books. All the doors fell off that and all the books fell out. You couldn't get out, you had to jump out the window. The girl I had with me at that stage had been in a fire in Auckland. She'd been caught in that fire and was absolutely petrified at this earthquake, so she jumped out the window and we couldn't find her. But we found her under a bed somewhere. I went under a bed. You can imagine, all the young girls had never been in an earthquake before — everybody got into everybody else's bed in one big room where there were a whole lot of beds, and we all stayed there the night.

Then they put us down into the Bristol Hotel in Ghuznee Street, and while we were there, there was a huge earthquake. The whole place rocked. Everybody ran out to the front steps inside the main door, and all the rats ran out from the kitchen, great big rats. The girls were screaming. But you get over those things — I mean people in England had bombs dropped, that was much worse. They said there was nowhere for us to go because the place in Molesworth Street hadn't been fixed up, so we just had to stay there. We did move back to Molesworth Street, because the Bristol Hotel was uninhabitable. It wasn't too long after that that I came back to Auckland.

Once you stopped being a runner, what did you do then?
There was an English squadron leader. I was taking some despatches to him and he said, 'I'm starting a new course. You look a nice little WAAF, would you like to go on that course? If you do well, you could go back to Auckland.' I said, 'Yes please.'

We had six weeks. We were three shifts, there were eight in each shift, and we all went through this course. I was good at maths, and it was all maths, so I flew through it. I think I got 100 per cent and I came top.

Queen Street, Masterton, showing the effects of the earthquake in June 1942. ATL, Evening Post Collection, G-123912-1/2

Did they tell you what it was for?

He said it was highly secret and we had to take an oath of secrecy before we went onto the course. That lasts for 50 years. We had to learn about radar, but we weren't trained in radar itself. We were trained in something called the filter room, which was the very secret part of it.

> *In February 1943, after finishing the course, Gwen was posted to Northern Group Headquarters*
> *in Epsom, which had been the teachers' training college.*

The operations room was one side and the filter room was the other. Nobody was allowed in the filter

*WAAFs in the plotting room at Northern Group Headquarters, Auckland,
July 1944.* RNZAF Official, via Air Force Museum, Christchurch, PR3658

room but our own personnel. We were connected directly to all the radar stations around the north of New Zealand. Unit 4 was at Piha; Unit 5 was at Waipapakauri; Unit 6 was at Spirits Bay; Unit 7 was at Whangarei Heads; and Unit 2 was at Hotwater Beach. I think Unit 3 was at New Plymouth, but we didn't have much to do with Unit 3. Unit 1 was at Motutapu, but that was a Army unit and we weren't connected with them. When the planes were coming in, all the stations would pick them up. It was the range that they were going on, and where all those ranges met, that's where the plane was. We would take that up to the gantry where they'd write it in a book, then they would pass it over to the operations room. Operations would put it on the table in the exact spot. After that we'd take the book. One person would be working on the map and you'd draw in the map where a plane was every 10 minutes. So you'd see whether they'd gone crooked or whether they were going straight.

They were supposed to have — and this was a secret part of it, too — IFF. IFF stood for 'Identification Friend or Foe'. The Americans didn't know where Auckland was and were very poor navigators, and sometimes they went right over Auckland as they came in. They'd go on to New Plymouth, and New

Plymouth would pick them up. Then we'd have to send a plane up and bring them back. Those boys would come in afterwards, because they wouldn't believe what had happened to them. On very special occasions they were allowed in to look at the maps to see where they had been. And because we'd saved their lives, because they would have gone off into the never-never, they were very thankful for that and would bring us nylons and candy.

How did you get the information from the radar stations?
That came by scrambled phone from every radar station.

> *There was one person for each telephone and the information they gathered was plotted on maps. The officers in the gantry looked down on the large maps and could see how each aircraft was going.*

It was often a male officer, but we also had a female officer roaming round with us. A lot of the officers would be men who were home on leave, who'd done a tour of duty and they were giving them a bit of a rest.

> *During this time, Gwen lived in a Waafery in Owens Road.*

It was on the side of Mt Eden in a big old home. There were eight bunks in each little room. Because we had to sleep at different times, we all had to have a place on our own, but you didn't get much sleep there because people kept wandering in to talk. The officers slept in a different room. We had a dining room in the old house, and they had showers out the back. I think we had to hand-wash our underwear and shirts and things. If we came off duty, and couldn't sleep, I would go home and have a sleep.

> *Gwen moved back to her parents' house when the Waafery became too crowded.*

I had to be down at headquarters at three o'clock in the morning, which was a bit frightening — nobody thought too much of it to start with, but it was quite frightening. If I saw anybody coming, I'd dodge in the hedges and gateways and crouch down and hide. There was another girl who lived further along,

Lynton Lodge, Owens Road, Epsom. The building on the right was used as a Waafery during the Second World War.
Special Collections, Auckland City Libraries, 7-A12114

and I'd go along and pick her up and we'd run down Poronui Street together. Then they decided that was too dangerous, so we'd go on duty at seven o'clock at night until seven o'clock in the morning. The whole shift would be there, but only three or four would be on duty. There'd be beds made up. You didn't get undressed, but you could lie in bed with a blanket over you unless there was an emergency, and then you were on duty.

We had a sergeant who stood at the front door of the headquarters, and we had to salute him every time we went in and every time we came out. He used to march us up and down the parade ground, so we learnt how to march and salute. I went on quite a few parades. We marched from the Domain right along Grafton Bridge, down Karangahape Road, down Queen Street, right down to the bottom. We did a few of those. There was a contingent of us, I suppose there would be 30 or 40 altogether.

Gwen vividly recalls the time when it seemed as though New Zealand was under imminent threat from a seaborne invasion.

They decided they'd give us a new table with a new map on it. Unit 6 had just come on the air and there was panic stations because they had picked up something just north of Cape Reinga. We were very tense — we thought we were going to be invaded any day — and they had picked up what they thought was an aircraft carrier, with aircraft flying around it. This is what came back to us. It was panic stations. We called all the heads of staff — the Army, the Navy, the Air Force and the Americans. All arrived in a great hurry. They were prancing around, and we were plotting all these planes and we had them going at 80 miles an hour. One of the officers got very upset and grabbed me by the shoulder and said, 'C'mon girl, what do they say now? What do they say now?' I looked at the map and I thought, I don't know, I think the Three Kings Islands are up there and they haven't drawn it on the map, so I said to him, 'Excuse me sir, but I think the Three Kings Islands are up there and it hasn't been drawn on the map.' I was the only Aucklander who knew the Three Kings Islands were there. They were very put out about that and there were many red faces. It happened two or three other times, because we were very nervous. We thought we were going to be invaded.

I know some people didn't like the Americans, but anybody who was here during the war thinks the Americans are pretty good, because if they hadn't come we would have been Japanese by now. They saved us, they really did. Being at Air Headquarters, I knew what was going on and how nervous they were. We didn't have much to be prepared with.

Gwen's father's firm, Henderson & Pollard, also became involved in the war effort, and it was because of this that Gwen came to know some American airmen.

We didn't have many aircraft here, and they wanted to pretend that we did, so they got Dad to make aircraft out of timber. They made a lot of those and put them round Hobsonville, hidden under trees so that if the Japanese did fly over they would have seen that we had planes there. My father would bring US airmen home. If I was there they'd sometimes say, 'Would you like to come out with me?' My niece was only three years younger than I was, so they'd take us both out. They were officers, so they took us to the Grand Hotel for dinner, which was very nice. They always took us by taxi. Then

US Marines are entertained by a New Zealand family. US National Archives

they'd take us to the Civic Theatre and we'd dance downstairs, to a band down there. They couldn't dance, but they were very nice.

We went to different dances in the services club in Queen Street and would meet the Americans there. I'd take them home sometimes and my mother would give them a meal. They were young. They were only 18, and they'd go over to the Islands and you'd never hear any more. They'd been killed. It was purely friendship. We were told we should be friendly to the Americans because how would you like it if your brother was overseas — you'd like somebody to befriend them. My mother was very good at doing that. She welcomed everybody into her home.

Was there ever any possibility of you going overseas?

Yes. They decided that the Japanese were coming too close for comfort and we really had to have a filter room up in the Islands. Our shift was the first shift and the most experienced, so they said, 'Would you be prepared to go?' At this time I was engaged to my future husband and he was not at all pleased. He didn't think that it was very good to have his wife going overseas, but I decided it was my duty and so I said I'd go. They gave me injections and I was very sick. We were all packed up, we were ready to go. The day before they said, 'No. We're winning now. We don't want you.' None of us went. We were going to Fiji.

Did it ever occur to you that the Allies wouldn't win?

Yes, it certainly did. We couldn't believe that Britain would be beaten, because she was invincible, but she nearly was. We were much more frightened of the Japanese, because they could have taken us. We didn't have any defences really, nothing, nothing at all. It really was quite scary at times, if you knew what I had known and you knew what was happening out there. You'd come off some mornings and there'd be 10 planes coming in. You didn't know who they were. Most of them were New Zealanders, but you didn't know. It was quite scary.

> *Gwen met her husband, Ronald Stevens, at the Crystal Palace ballroom in 1944. He was in the Army's transport unit. The couple became engaged and were married in 1945. They had a son and a daughter. Gwen, now a widow, is closely involved with the ex-servicewomen's group of the Howick RSA.*

Every year at the cenotaph at Stockade Hill, we march on Anzac Day and lay a wreath. Then we march down — there are not many of us, and we lead the parade. The band, the flag-bearers, and then there's us. We salute the dignitaries on the way down. I think there are about 30 of us still.

'WE WERE VERY GOOD SHOTS'

George CLARK, Home Guard

Working on the family farm, George Clark was in a reserved occupation, so his war service was in the Home Guard. George was born in Hamilton in 1922 and grew up at Te Pahu in the Waikato, near Mt Pirongia. He and his brother attended the small country school at Kaniwhaniwha before being sent to Auckland by their parents, Elizabeth and Fred, to attend Mt Albert Grammar.

When you were growing up, were you expected to do chores on the farm?

It wasn't a question of being expected, you just did them. It was our job to catch the horses in the morning, harness them to the sledge and take the cream down the road to where the cream lorry came. At school we let the horses go in the horse paddock, then caught the horses afterwards and brought the empty cans home at night.

During the Depression of the 1930s there was a Public Works camp near the Clark farm.

The people at the camp lived in tents. One day, all the camp bread had been put in the cream cans and we drove the cans to the camp just below our house. We were taking the lid off the can and it must have startled the horses a wee bit. The horses started to trot up the road, the can fell off and the bread spread all

Left: *Relief workers at a public works camp, Akatarawa, near Wellington.* ATL, Evening Post Collection, G-84256-1/2

Previous page: *Members of the Paraparaumu Home Guard outside the local hall.* ATL, New Zealand Free Lance Collection, PAColl-8602-42
Top: *George Clark.* George Clark collection

up the road. We put the bread back in the cans and took it to the camp. They didn't mind.

What were they doing, those men?

They were metalling the roads. There was a certain amount of metal that they got out of the creeks, but then that dried up and they did this manoeuvre that you would call 'tap and turn' — one fella held a long rod with a cutter on the end and another fella would tap it and turn it till he got down in the limestone far enough and then they'd blow it. Then they got the horses and drays and dumped it on the roads, and the men had to knap it with their big rock hammers. It was a slow process.

Some of the wives lived with the men in the camp. Today you'd be aghast if you saw where they spent winters, but you never heard them complain.

George's two paternal uncles were in the First World War.

One got killed on Gallipoli and the other died of influenza in England, just a week before he was due to go over to France in the Medical Corps. My father joined up, too, but they sent him home. They said [to his parents], 'You've got two sons over there. I think that's sufficient.' He was still willing to go. I can't understand it. As we were brought up, we were told all about the First World War, hearing the stories from our parents, so I would never have gone willingly. I would have gone if we'd been called. My father had a neighbour down the road, Mr Steele, and he was a sniper during the First World War. I can remember going down to my father's farm to work, and you'd hear them talking about the war.

What effect did that have on your grandparents — two sons being killed, or dying?

I think my old grandfather had a fortitude second to none. I would think he kept everything inside, but I know when Frank got killed in Gallipoli my grandmother had a stroke and she really never recovered from that. When the boy died of influenza before he went to France they didn't want to tell her, and she kept saying, 'Where's my Herbert?' all the time. She never really recovered. I remember even in our day the mothers talking about when the horrendous losses from Gallipoli came out. The country was shocked about what was happening.

In 1936, George and his brother Tom were sent to Mt Albert Grammar.

Minister of Defence Fred Jones inspecting Wellington College cadets.
ATL, Evening Post Collection, PAColl-8557-43

We'd left this little school down home with, say, 13 pupils, and we went up to Mt Albert. There were 650 there. I'm one of these people who can bottle everything up, because no tears ever got out of my eyes. The thing was to get home. We had our school calendars and sometimes we'd mark off every day as it went, and some days we'd let three days go by so we could mark three off in a row. We knew our parents and grandparents, in the slump, had done a lot to put us into school. My grandfather, I think, was the instigator. His two brothers who were lost in the war, we've got records of them and they were very well-educated, so education meant a lot to the family.

Was there a cadet corps there?
Yes, we used to go every Wednesday afternoon, and we even had uniforms with those lemon-squeezer hats. The socks they gave us didn't have any toe in them. There was just something that went between your big toe and the sock, and they were the most uncomfortable things in the world to wear. They were horrible! We marched around on the field to the drum. I never got shooting practice at school. Sometimes I think we felt like toy soldiers.

In 1942, George's brother Tom went into camp. He served in the Pacific for around two years.

I was called up like all the others, but of course you can't take both the workers off a farm, so I was left home on the farm. It didn't worry me one way or the other.

So you weren't one of these young men who had a burning ambition to get away overseas?
I never joined them in that. We knew the horrors of war. We knew what our grandparents suffered, and our parents. My mother's brother was killed in France. We knew all about war and the misery. Loyalty to your country — I know it's good. If you have to go, you go; but if you didn't have to go, I wouldn't.

Do you think you were patriotic?
Of course we were patriotic, of course. We started off with loyalty to our parents, then loyalty to your country. I think that loyalty stayed with me all my life.

Tell me about the Home Guard, how did you hear about that?
To be quite honest, I don't know. The Home Guard was formed — I don't know who formed it — and we found out that you went down to the hall every Saturday. I hadn't realised until I started to read through

my old diaries that we went down there at about 11 o'clock and there was a lunch provided for us. There might have been a lecture before lunch. Sometimes we got there in time for the lecture and sometimes we didn't. It was a question of what was happening on the farm at the time. I see in the diaries that some

Christchurch South Home Guardsmen practising signalling. ATL, War History Collection, DA-03315

days we'd gone out and dagged a few sheep or drenched some lambs, and then gone off to Home Guard. The two had to work together. If you couldn't go, you couldn't go. I missed a hand grenade shoot because we were doing something that day. It could have been haymaking, could have been shearing.

Was it just you from your family?

No, my father always went too, and my brother, Tom, before he was called up. I remember one day, Tom had been in camp for a little while and we'd come down to the hall and they were having some combat exercises. Tom said, 'A fella can charge me and I can disarm you easily.' An old dairy farmer said, 'I don't believe that's possible.' So he ran at Tom with his gun — it didn't have a bayonet on — and the next thing he was flipped on his back. He looked up and said, 'I didn't think that was possible.' Little unarmed combat things.

We used to have exercises. We were out on a night patrol and were told to guard a certain section while these other fellas, from another platoon, had to walk past. I was standing there in the pitch-black dark and this old farmer came walking along. He was one of the enemy. He walked right past me. I could have put my hand out and touched him. He was looking so cunning as he walked past. I don't know why I let him go past. I think I might have given him a heart attack if I'd grabbed him. If the real thing was on, we had strangling wire. It was a loose wire you'd slip over a person's head and pull tight. We were issued with those things. If it had been the real thing, he didn't stand a chance, that old farmer. I never told him how close he was. He thought he'd done a great deal, getting past. I was a bit naughty, I suppose I should have apprehended him. We had a lot of fun along the way.

One day, as an exercise, my father and I were told to go up and do a night patrol and watch a certain house to see the movement. There was nothing suspicious in the house. We sat up on this cold hillside in the frosty night for quite a lot of hours and had to report no movement.

You didn't mind doing those sorts of things?

It didn't worry us. We did all sorts of exercises. One day they'd organised a hike from our side of the mountain over to Oparau. Two of my uncles thought it was a pity to go through all that bush and not do some hunting, so they brought their pig dogs along, and on the way over they caught two or three pigs. A bit of pleasure with work.

Home Guard members at rest during an exercise. ATL, Evening Post Collection, PAColl-8557-46

They had a road block on the old mountain road where they had big concrete abutments built and a big rimu log they were going to roll down if the Japanese came through that way. On our side, looking down the Waitetuna Valley, we dug a dugout on top of the hill. I don't think we spent a lot of time up there, but we certainly had a good observation point.

When you've only got a rifle and 10 rounds of ammunition it wouldn't have gone far, and my brother poked a bit of a hole in our ability when he said, 'If anything really happens the Army will be here that quickly, you won't be needed.'

We had a major, he was a good old chap, but I remember we were walking to our lookout and I said to my uncle, 'If anything happens, Uncle Tom, we're not going to take any notice of that silly old fella, are we?' He said, 'Of course not. We'll just do what we have to do.' My uncle was a sergeant. Another old chap, a Scotsman, a farmer down the road, was the sergeant-major. He was

Members of the Home Guard have a tea break. ATL, Evening Post Collection, PAColl-8557-48

quite a plump old boy and I heard my uncle say he looked like one of those ads for Michelin tyres. Another fella was appointed a captain. It was a loose formation. I would like to think we behaved ourselves reasonably well. You had to have some sort of an organisation.

If you'd done something wrong, could they punish you for it?
I don't think they'd have got very far. You had to have some sort of discipline, and I think most people took it OK. My uncle was supposed to have done something naughty, so they decided to fine him about five shillings. It didn't take long to pass the hat round to pay for the fine.

We had a rifle range on a farm down the road which we used. We did a lot of shooting. We had a Springfield rifle which they issued. We had 10 rounds of ammunition to take home. The army used to come out and give us very good instruction on machine guns and trench mortars. If they ever wanted us to do drill they didn't have much luck, but they showed us how to blow railway tracks with gelignite. They were very good at that. I don't think we took it seriously enough because we had other things to do.

How many of you would there have been in that Home Guard unit?
About 20 or 30 of us. One day we were down at the hall and one of my aunties rang up and said there was a wild pig on her farm. They had some sows there running in the fern around the place, so we got our rifles and raced up to the farm. I saw this big black object walking through the fern and I was just about to fire at it when my uncle said, 'Don't fire, don't fire! It might be one of my sows.' I reckon I could have nailed that boar.

A Home Guard unit on patrol in the bush near Wellington. ATL, John Pascoe Collection, F-16-1/4

We had uniforms. I don't know if we wore them every time we went down to the hall. Silly little hats. I don't think we ever wore them, they made a farmer look quite strange really. They'd issued us with some Army boots, light boots. There was a game of rugby one day against another platoon from somewhere, and my rugby boots from school were a bit ancient by then so I played in these Army boots. Halfway through the game, the sole came off one boot. They couldn't have been very good quality.

We had flags for signalling. That was quite interesting. We had our rifles and our strangling wire. We used to have exercises in trying to judge distances. We were taught that if you could see a man and you couldn't see his arms, you'd know he'd be a certain distance away. The Army, the professional soldiers, were very efficient.

How long would you be there on Saturdays?
Sometimes through till five o'clock. We'd get home in time to milk the cows. Most of them would end by about four o'clock.

George recalls a manoeuvre where his group had to capture a ridge from another Home Guard unit on Mt Pirongia.

Members of the Home Guard with packs. ATL, War History Collection, PAColl-5547-079

We went over the old mountain road to a certain point. We had to cross a big bush gully and go up the other side — we were supposed to be the surprise party. We navigated our way quite well and got up the other side, and the first thing we knew, a scout came. They had scouts down this ridge as though they were expecting us to be there. We had flour bombs. I never had the chance to throw mine, but I know I was crawling up through this scrub and there was a fella right on top of me, so if it had been the real thing I wouldn't have lasted long. Anyhow, some of the others caught some of the scouts and made them carry their gear up to the top. When we got to the top, another group of ours had gone round and come in the back and overpowered them. We were sort of the bait. We'd left the cars up the top and had to walk all the way back up the road again.

You used your own transport to get around?

Yes.

Did you get a special petrol ration for that?

Not that I know of. They rationed butter, but we made our own off the farm. A young fella came down one day and said, 'Do you want a bag of sugar?' We said, 'What? You can't get us a bag.' He said, 'Of course I can.' He lived in Auckland. Came down one day with a bag of sugar. I guess it was black-market.

You couldn't get tyres for your cars. We'd tried. A lady down the road said she'd filled in a questionnaire and told the whole truth and she didn't get any tyres. Anyhow, we gave our questionnaire to the cream lorry driver. He said, 'I'll get you a tyre. Just fill it in.' The tyre arrived on the tank stand the next morning. A little bit of that went on.

Petrol rationing had little effect on their farm work.

In those days we ploughed with horses. Sometimes petrol got a bit short to go to a dance. We had an old truck and we'd apply for some petrol to do some harrowing on the farm, but I'm afraid the petrol never got into the paddock. We used to attend a lot of chopping events in those days. You had to do something.

George recalls that movies were also shown in the local hall.

My father used to go down. I was always too tired to bother to go.

Did people think the Japanese were going to come?

Oh yes. We men were going to survive because we could have gone bush, but then you've got your grandparents, and mothers and young children at home. That was a big worry. It was real enough, but we did what we could and the Army helped us along. I think we probably knew more about the bush than the instructors. We'd hunted pigs all our lives and tramped over the mountain. We knew how to shoot well, we were very good shots, actually. I always thought I was the crack shot of the Home Guard — I got very good reports.

Did you have strong feelings about Germans?

Unfortunately, yes, because of losing three uncles in the First World War. The Germans were known as 'Huns' and 'the Boche', and stories came back from the First World War. As young people we sort of hated the Germans because of that, but later on in life you realise that the Germans were probably just like us. They no more wanted to fight us than we wanted to fight them, but a German meant war to us when we were young. Our honest opinion was that we felt sorry for the Germans getting led into another world war. Very sad for the German people. And the world. A close neighbour of ours was a German fella. He was a good guy, patriotic. He was in the Home Guard and nothing was ever done about that, which I'm pleased about.

We thought the Italians weren't warlike. A different type of people from the Germans. We learnt more about the Japanese after the war, and I'm afraid that even today I don't want to buy a Japanese car because of the atrocities they committed. They were badly led too. We didn't hear a lot about the Japanese. We heard about their ravages in China, so we knew that they weren't what you'd call British gentlemen type. I don't necessarily dislike a nation as a whole, but you dislike the leaders and the people who led their people astray. Wars prove nothing.

Did it ever occur to you that the Allies wouldn't win?

Never! It was only a question of time. I never doubted for a moment that we would win but, by Jove, I still think that the Americans saved us. We did know one American. He was a deserter and lived with a woman down the road for quite some time.

As the war went on and it seemed less likely there'd be an invasion by the Japanese, did your Home Guard duties wind down?

We kept going for a while. They came out eventually and took the rifles away, and much later they came and took the uniforms. When the uniforms went back I got a little account — apparently I hadn't returned a field dressing — of one shilling and sevenpence. They said I could send a cheque to such-and-such an address. Bureaucracy was still strong.

George did not send the cheque. The family also had to battle bureaucracy regarding George's brother, Tom, who had returned from the Pacific suffering from hepatitis, hookworm and malaria.

George and Margaret Clark on their wedding day, 1949. George Clark collection

The officialdom wanted to send him to another farm, when we needed him on our farm. It was so stupid. We were short-handed all during the war years. In fact, most of those war years, on a Sunday I went and had a sleep under a tree somewhere. I was always tired. I got up at ten to five in the morning and might finish at seven to half past seven at night. They were long days.

George and Tom had inherited their grandfather's farm after his death in 1942. Eventually George bought Tom out. In 1946, he met Margaret MacMurray, who had come to do her country teaching service at Te Pahu. The couple married in 1949 and have four daughters. In 1987 they retired to the Bay of Plenty, where they still live.

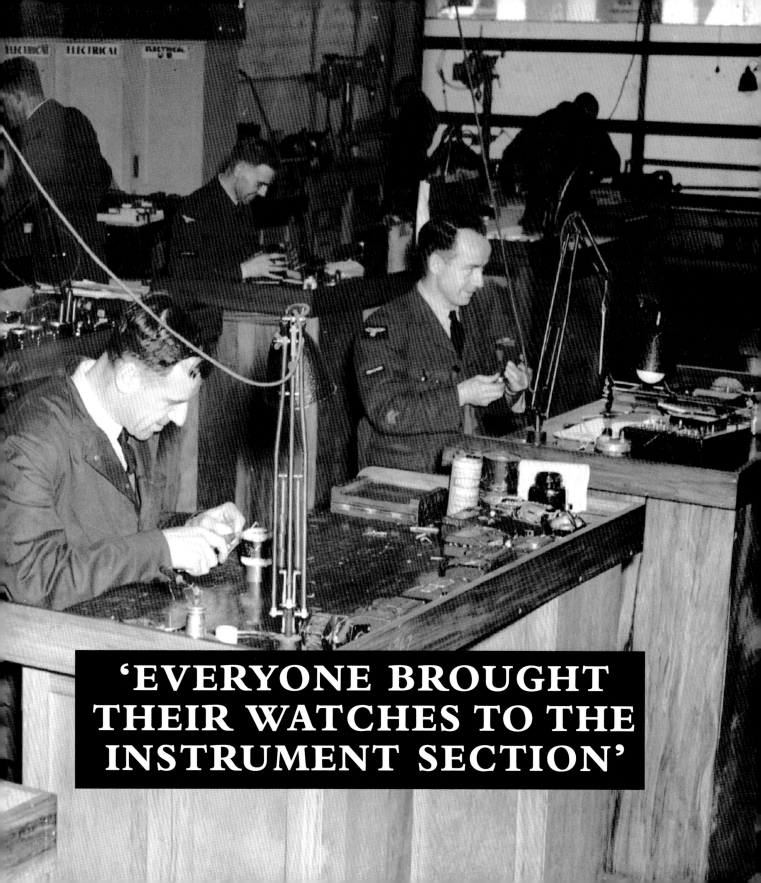

'EVERYONE BROUGHT THEIR WATCHES TO THE INSTRUMENT SECTION'

Peter CRISPE, 4310874,
Aircraftsman 1st Class, RNZAF

Peter, the son of Colin and Joanna Crispe, was born in Clevedon, near Auckland, in 1926.

I WAS BORN IN THE SCHOOL HOUSE. Dad was headmaster of Clevedon School. We had a car accident when I was nearly five. We were going in to Auckland to see Father Christmas at the Farmers Parade. Dad had filled up with petrol at the garage in Clevedon and was moving slowly out onto the loose metal road. He was bending down and winding the clock — you had to put your hand right under the dashboard to wind the winder — and he hit a big rock on the side of the road. He was going quite slowly, but steered the car into a telegraph pole. I was sitting in the front seat, and I had 11 pieces of glass in my forehead. I was yelling my head off. They took me to Dr Walls in Clevedon. I was still making a lot of noise and the dear old doctor produced his gold hunter watch, held it out and said, 'Blow on it, boy. Blow on it!' I blew hard and he pushed the button and the lid flew open and I could see the face and the hands. I'm sure my interest in watches and clocks stems from that occasion.

In 1933, Peter and his family travelled to the United Kingdom to visit family. There he attended a preparatory school in Northern Ireland belonging to his aunt and uncle. After a year the family returned to New Zealand and Peter was sent to King's School as a boarder. It was while he was there that his hearing deteriorated and so his mother moved him to Manurewa School, which he attended up to Standard 6.

Previous page: *No. 1 Repair Depot Instrument Repair section personnel at work, Hamilton, 1944.* RNZAF Official, via Air Force Museum, Christchurch, HamG648
Above: *Peter Crispe, August 1943.* Peter and Heather Crispe collection

Then we had a bit of a time to try and find a secondary school that would take a deaf boy. King's College wouldn't look at me. Our ear, nose and throat specialist, Dr James Hardie-Neil, who was married to my mother's cousin, said, 'I know Gerry Park, who runs Seddon Tech and I'm sure I can organise you to have your schooling there.' And that was what happened. I did three marvellous years, 1940–43, at Tech, and I enjoyed every moment

Seddon Memorial Technical School, Wellesley Street, Auckland. ATL, Auckland Star Collection, G-2932-1/1

of it. I worked in the electrical lab, which was very much to my liking. I took engineering. All the teachers were wonderful to me. I had to sit up the front. The other kids used to call me 'teachers' pet'.

In 1943, I'd passed the public service entrance exam and my form master, Mr Webber — he was known as 'Spider' Webber — was the OC of the ATC squadron I was in, and he said to me, 'I can't really see you working in a telephone exchange or anything like that. There's a war on, and at 17, with

Men line up to enlist in the Rutland Street drill hall. Special Collections, Auckland City Libraries, A13149

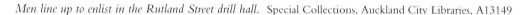

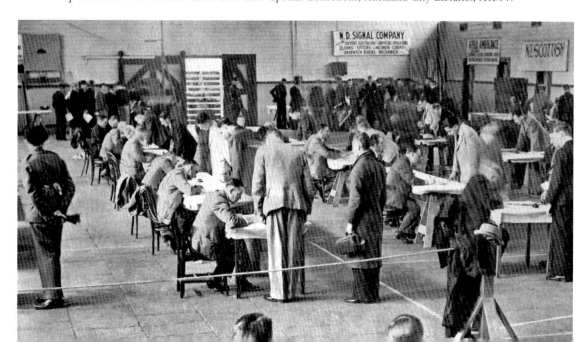

15 months in the ATC, you can volunteer as a boy entrant.' And I volunteered. I went down to the drill hall for a medical and they discovered my hearing wasn't very good. As luck would have it, Dr Hardie-Neil was the ear, nose and throat specialist for the drill hall in Rutland Street in Auckland, and they sent me up to him with the form. I knew his house very well as I'd lived in it when I was first at Tech, instead of travelling out to Manurewa every day. I marched into his surgery — he didn't have anyone there — and put the form in front of him. He put his glasses on and looked at it and he said, 'Air Force? You?' I said, 'Yes.' He signed his name just like that. Said to me, 'Do you good to get away from mum for a bit', and that was it.

It was a complete medical for everything. I was quite fit, apart from the hearing.

What did your mother think about your idea of joining the Air Force?
She was all for it. She was in a very patriotic frame of mind altogether. 'My goodness,' she said, 'if that's what you're going to do, you've got my signature.' Dad didn't hesitate either. When I first spoke of it to Mum, she said, 'Go for it, go for it. It'll be the making of you.' Which was only too true, really.

I went from Auckland with a contingent of boys my own age on the Limited down to Wellington, and they picked us up and took us to Rongotai. Huge dormitories in Rongotai. We were going across to Blenheim to the Delta camp, near Woodbourne. We were up early the next morning and told to put a good shine on our shoes and our buttons and everything, and to our amazement found we were marching in a Savings for Victory parade in Wellington. I think we missed lunch, because when the parade ended we were trucked straight away along the quay to get on the ferry to go to Picton.

When we arrived at Picton, it was about half past nine at night, and we found that the train to Blenheim only had one complete passenger carriage and one guard's van, and there were 60 of us. They packed us all, standing up, into the guard's van. I remember a chap standing next to me who I didn't know. I was feeling round in my greatcoat pocket. Mum had secreted all sorts of things there — there were bars of chocolate and so forth — and I found this lovely bar of chocolate and broke it in half and gave half to this chap next to me. His name was Quentin Alexander Robb, and we're still friends to this day.

We arrived at Blenheim station. There were a load of trucks waiting to shift us out to Delta. It was after 10 o'clock at night by then. They had the mess going, and as we were served our various dishes all along the mess, I can remember the chaps behind the counter saying, 'You'll be sorry. You'll be sorry. You'll be sorry.' It was a very common expression in the forces for new recruits.

Airmen eating Christmas dinner at the Delta camp, 1943. RNZAF Official, via Air Force Museum, Christchurch, PR2411

We were just about to tuck in, and all of a sudden there was a stentorian shout from the flight sergeant and Flight Lieutenant Barnes, the commandant of the camp, jumped onto one of the tables and bawled at us. 'You're now in the Air Force and you'll do as you're told! Reveille's at six a.m. in the morning and woe betide anyone that's still in his bed at five past! There are cold showers available.'

We were then issued with the wherewithal for our three-man huts, which consisted of a straw palliasse, a sheet, two blankets, and that was it. It was August in the Wairau Valley, very cold. Coming from Auckland, we were really feeling the cold, but we all settled in there extraordinarily well.

The next day we were up being checked over and issued with a .303 each. The idea was that as ground staff we had to be able to defend an aerodrome if necessary. During the six weeks, we did everything: a couple of nights' camp out in the bush, fired a Bren gun, threw a live grenade, and went through a gas chamber. It only had tear gas in it. We had to take our masks off inside to experience it, and put them on again.

Peter has vivid memories of Corporal Tyrell at the Delta camp.

He was a small man but he had a tremendous voice. He was always so smart. His battledress was ironed with creases like knife edges in the sleeves of his jacket and in his pants, and you could see your face in his boots and his buttons, they shone so much. He wouldn't stand any nonsense or fiddling around at all. He alarmed us all and had us wondering, What will the corporal think? I remember one of his expressions — he had us all standing to attention and a lot were wobbling around, and in his best voice he said, 'Stand still, damn you! You're like a lot of fairies fidgeting and farting around.' That was a bit of a shock to me, because my father had never said anything like that to me. I remember my mother scrubbing my mouth out with soap and water because I said 'bum'.

Was there much swearing among the other boys?
Not really. There were one or two that swore quite a lot, but we didn't really come across a lot of swearing until we got out into the Air Force proper.

We had all put down an issue that we liked the idea of and the type of section we'd like to join. Some wanted to be aircrew. I knew that with my hearing I couldn't manage that, but I was interested in the radio or the instrument section. I pushed a bit to go to Wigram to the wireless school, but they were absolutely full up. The education officer said to me, 'Instrument repair will probably be the best for you.' And with that we were sent to the preliminary technical training school in Rongotai in Wellington.

There we did an engineering course in about six weeks. It was the absolute replica of my schooldays course at Seddon Tech, so I just waltzed through it. I didn't have to do any homework or anything. I knew the mechanics and the science and I was very handy with files and drills. I got something like 85 per cent when I went through that course. Those who got the higher marks went to be instrument

Opposite: *RNZAF Technical Training School in the former Centennial Exhibition building at Rongotai.*
ATL, W.H. Raine Collection, G-21676-1/1

Peter Crispe (front row, with bugle) at the instrument repair school in Hamilton, December 1943.
Peter and Heather Crispe collection

repairers. The next highest were engine fitters, and then airframe repairers. I think if you were under 50 per cent you could be an aircraft hand, general duties, which meant you could be either in the kitchen or scrubbing out the loos.

During the course there was this infamous Christmas strike. All the people on the station, a lot of them in the PTTS, were denied Christmas leave. They got together and decided that it was a very poor thing that they shouldn't get the time off, although someone kept saying, 'There's a war on. You can't expect the holidays.' They arranged it that on morning parade that particular morning all the markers would march out, because they could be individually identified by the warrant officer. When the markers were all on spot we were given the order to parade and nobody moved. An Air Commodore came from the Air Ministry to harangue us about it all, telling us about his son who was on operations somewhere overseas, but they relented and allowed us to have a few days off at Christmas after all. Our actual PTTS course didn't start, I think, until the beginning of the new year, so we were hanging around with nothing much to do. They found lots of things for us to sweep, like the parade ground.

It was during that time that they discovered that I didn't always hear the orders when I was on parade. They were looking through my files and found that I'd been a trumpeter and a bugler at Seddon Tech, so they put me with a very nice chap who was in his late fifties, I would think. His name was Johnson, and he taught me the trumpet without any keys, and all the Air Force calls for the general salute to blow the flag up in the morning at eight o'clock. The orderly officer and the orderly sergeant pulled the flag up and there'd be two trumpeters — at Rongotai, there were three — and we blew the general salute together, and then the 'Carry on' after that. The rest of the group would go for a route march, but we trumpeters returned to our barracks, presumably for trumpet practice. It meant that the barracks that I was in never got a black mark from the orderly officer's daily inspection, because I was back after my trumpet call and I would straighten up anyone's uniform that wasn't in the right place, or a drawer which had been left open or something like that, and made sure that we never got a black mark.

You said that you learnt the Air Force calls for the trumpet. Does that mean they were different from the Army ones?

Yes. We still used the 'Last Post' for funerals, and the reveille too, but the Air Force general salute for blowing up the flag was different, as was the 'Alert' and the 'Carry on' afterwards too. We had our trumpet on our right hip, held up halfway, and the salute was just to put it slightly down, parallel to the ground, and bring it up again. That was how you saluted the officer. When I got to Hamilton, to the instrument school, I was station trumpeter there. And after I finished the instrument school, at Ardmore I was station trumpeter there. In 1945, when I went down to Rukuhia, they didn't have a parade ground. I did the odd funeral, but not daily like I'd been used to doing.

> *After the preliminary technical training course at Rongotai, Peter was sent to the instrument repair school at Hamilton for six weeks.*

There were a number of very good instructors and they taught us different areas. Physical instruments — ones operated by temperature or air pressure — and electrical instruments. A lovely chap called Les Hall took us for gyroscopic theory. We learnt all about the rate of climb indicators, and the turn and bank ones.

We did some very careful work there. We had to make a little lock that would go in a cabinet or a drawer or a door, make it all out of metal, and we had to file it to very close tolerances. I got good marks off that section, and that was when I was moved up to AC1. Every class we went to, we made notes and then wrote them up in the evening. They examined those.

There were about 30 men on the course.

Several of them had gone with me to the Delta camp. There were some lovely characters amongst them.

There was a lot of American stuff coming in by then. My course notebook mentions all the American styles of instrument. There was a marked difference between the English aircraft and the American ones. There were still Oxfords and Ansons. I think they used to call the Oxford the 'flying glasshouse' because it had so many windows on it. It had twin engines and we had to go up in them sometimes to adjust some of the instruments in flight. To start them, you had to get up on the wing and put a crank handle through a hole in the wing and crank it round, and they operated the switch for ignition, and it started. You had to pull your crank handle out, and close the orifice where it went in, and the propeller was threatening to blow you off the wing. You slid down on the wing and got back in the door.

Did you have your own toolkit?

They were Air Force property. We were issued with a bunch of tools, and then when we were transferred to another station, we had to hand that one in and get another one from the next station. A lot of us, as we went on, started getting our own tools together. We found some of the things weren't very suitable. Some of the English stuff was rough compared to what the Americans had. The American instruments were beautiful tools.

After the instrument school, Peter was a fully-fledged 'instrument basher'. He was posted to No. 5 Servicing Unit at Ardmore airfield, near Auckland.

We were a servicing unit for pilots that were training for oxygen use before they went up to the Islands. The instrument repairers had to recharge the oxygen tanks. It meant we had our own tractor and an oxygen tank that was 15, 16 feet long and about 15 inches in diameter. We'd go round to each aircraft and

A group of pilots pose with a Corsair, Ardmore, 1945. RNZAF Official, via Air Force Museum, Christchurch, PR6870

check the onboard tanks for pressure, and if there was insufficient we would hook up our tank into it.

One ghastly thing happened there. They all looked the same, the gas bottles, but they had different painted rings on them showing what they were. Somehow or other, an acetylene bottle got painted with oxygen marks on it, and I think three or four kites got topped up with acetylene. The commander of the flight was one. He turned his oxygen on before the others and started feeling so queer about it, he took it off and said to the others, 'Put it on, but if you feel odd, take it off.' He very nearly crashed, but managed to pull out in time. There was hell to pay at the court of inquiry into how it had happened. Someone in the stores had done something wrong and painted the wrong mark on the bottle.

It was nearly all Kittyhawks. They were the most-used American plane in those days, but before I left Ardmore the first Corsair arrived. One of the things about Ardmore that they had to be careful about was that it was built on a swamp, and if a Kittyhawk or a Corsair ran off the runway, the ground was so soft the wheels sank straight in and usually the tail would come up and they'd bury the prop in the mud. I think a Corsair weighed 30 tons, and when that happened with a Corsair, the pilot was trapped about 18 feet above his propeller. He couldn't get down. They had to put an extra large ladder on the crash tender to rescue them. They had a double nine, 18-cylinder engine — two banks of nine cylinders. They were almost capable of the speed of sound in a dive, the Corsairs.

I was in the Number 5 SU and they wanted more in the headquarters section, so I moved there. That's where I met Flight Sergeant Adrian Timewell, who'd been a watchmaker in Wyndham Street in Auckland before the war. I could see him observing this new boy, and as time went on he became friendly. After about three or four months in that instrument shop, he said to me, 'When the war's over, I'm going to start the first jeweller's shop in Papatoetoe, and I'm hoping you'll come and be my apprentice there.' He'd been apprenticed in 1926 and used to do repairs for all sorts of jewellers as well as people who came into the shop. Amongst other things, one of his specialities was taxi meters. In the pre-war days, they were all mechanical and full of gears, run by a flexible drive from a wheel. He used to tell me that when they arrived at work on Monday mornings, there'd be at least three taxis outside with broken-down meters to fix.

He was a man of great experience. Of course he had absolutely the right name for it. He taught me so much, and he was so patient. If I broke something, he wasn't cross. He had one bad fault: he smoked endlessly. He lit one cigarette from the one he'd finished. He'd have a Nescafé tin on the bench with a hole punched in it and he'd smoke cigarettes right down to the butt and drop them in that. When he was repairing watches, he'd have a cigarette in his mouth and the smoke would be trickling up the sides of his face. His top lip was quite yellow from smoking.

He was a lifelong friend. He was a brilliant watchmaker and he taught me so much. Even now, I sit at my bench and I'm doing a particular thing and I say to myself, 'That's how Timey used to do it.' He was very highly thought of in the instrument world in Ardmore. Nothing went wrong with his instruments, they were always absolutely spot-on, and the engineer officers used to confer with him a lot over any problems they had. Such an accident of joining the Air Force and then running into someone who could affect your whole life like that. From blowing on the doctor's watch to meeting Adrian Timewell, it's just never stopped.

> *After five or six months at Ardmore, Peter was posted to Rukuhia, at Mystery Creek near Hamilton.*

Squadron Leader Kingsford was the commander of No. 1 Airframe Repair Unit. Actually, when I went there it was called Airframe Repair Section and all the overalls we wore in the hangars had *No. 1 ARS*

Left: *Adrian Timewell at Wigram, 1940.* Peter and Heather Crispe collection
Below: *Members of the instrument section at Rukuhia. Peter Crispe is at front right.* Peter and Heather Crispe collection

on them and of course, being what they are, every one of them had an 'e' added on to it. Squadron Leader Kingsford was very upset about this when he came and so he had the name of the unit changed to Airframe Repair Unit.

Nearly all the transport aircraft came there for fitting. Loads of DC3s. They've got a sort of bonnet in front of the window which opens like a car bonnet. They used to put up a tripod ladder and I'd go up there. They'd open the bonnet, I'd get in, and they'd close it. I had to put a new filter in the automatic pilot. It was run on hydraulic oil, the filter. You had to have the engines running and the oil coming through and the connections loose so that all the air would be blown out of it. As soon as you saw fluid coming out both ends, you quickly screwed them up and tightened them up. It took me about 10 minutes to do that with both engines running. Then they did all the other tests on the engines, like testing the magnetos and running them up, and I'd be 25 minutes, half an hour, stuck up in this thing until they'd turned the engines off. I never think that did much for my hearing.

We always had to be careful about the clocks in the aircraft. If there was a crash, after they'd removed the bodies the first person in had to be an instrument repairer to take the clock out, because clocks were number one loot amongst all the aircraftmen. If there was a chance of getting away with the clocks, then they went. It used to be horrifying to do a daily inspection on the aircraft and find someone had pinched the clock. With the Phillips-type screws we used, we used to drill out the projections in them so they couldn't unscrew them. Some of the pilots unscrewed them in the air and took off with them.

At the last of the war they were flying in aircraft from the Islands that they parked all round the airfield at Rukuhia. There would be about 10 planes come in with ferry pilots from the Islands, and there'd be a DC3 waiting for the ferry pilots. They'd park them around the field and we instrument repairers had to be out quickly and get the clocks out of those. There must have been a couple of hundred aircraft all parked around the edge of the field.

What happened to those aircraft?
They were broken up in the end. There were people called Valentine, I think, in Hamilton — they got the hydraulic legs and that sort of thing, and made farm equipment out of them. They melted down an

Opposite: *15 Squadron pilots run to their P-40 Kittyhawks at Whenuapai, 1942.* RNZAF Official, via Air Force Museum, Christchurch, PR190

enormous amount of aluminium and so forth. There was a firm just across the road with a garage that bought a lot of the aircraft and dismantled them. You could buy all sorts of things.

Did you have a favourite aircraft to work on?

Yes. I always liked the Kittyhawks. One of the things they had was a rev counter that counted the revolutions of the engine. It was quite a big instrument on the right-hand side of the panel. It had a short flexible cable that went through a couple of bulkheads into the camshaft at the back of the engine. On the 80-hour inspection, I think, we had to take that out and clean the inner part that did the spinning, and clean the outer, and carefully re-grease it and put it all back in the engine. I remember on one occasion I put too much grease in the flexible drive, and the way it was spinning forced all the grease back into the instrument and filled the instrument up. Fortunately, they discovered it when they were running it up on the ground. It didn't take off. I had a mild reprimand: 'Be a bit gentle on the grease next time.'

Everyone on the station brought their watches to the instrument section. It was full of watchmakers. At Rukuhia, the majority of them were watchmakers. There was one chap in particular, Eric Bulmer, who was very skilled. He used to get more than he could do, and he sort of half-apprenticed me and got me doing easy jobs, like putting a new mainspring in and that sort of stuff. Everyone from the commanding officer down to the cooks took their watches to the instrument section.

It was a funny time of life altogether, really. It seemed so nice and peaceful — wartime equipment all round you, and yet it didn't seem as though anything could happen. When you came into Auckland and you saw the gun turrets around St Heliers and all that, it was quite something.

I remember there were cheers all through Rukuhia when VE Day came, and they were saying, 'How long will it be before we knock the Japs?' When the news came through of the surrender and of the Hiroshima and Nagasaki bombs, everyone absolutely cheered in the unit. The first thing that people started saying was, 'I wonder how soon we can get discharged, now it's over?' Everyone was just aching to get out. 'I've done the war. I want to get out now.' Some of them who had coral cuts on their legs from the Islands had to go up to Auckland Hospital and have them dressed every day, and they wouldn't discharge them until they were properly healed. You had to go back into civvy life in perfect order. The MO was very worried about me and my hearing, but I truthfully said, 'Oh, I was deaf when I went in.' One of my friends who was behind me said, 'You were a mug. You should have said you'd gone deaf in service and you would have got a pension.'

After the war, Peter served a four-year apprenticeship with Adrian Timewell under the rehabilitation scheme, instead of the usual five years. In 1950, he went to London with a letter of introduction to the British Horological Institute and got a job with Charles Frodsham & Co., the royal watch- and clockmakers. He worked there for five years, and then spent three years with British European Airways. On 9 January 1954, he married Heather Jerram.

Our fathers were boys together, and I met Heather in 1943 when she was going into the Navy and I was going into the Air Force. I didn't meet her again until 1953. Mother said to me, 'I want you to come to my flat on my birthday. Heather Jerram's come over for the coronation. I'm going to have her there as well.' I breezed into Mum's flat in Baker Street in London, and here was this lovely fair-haired girl sitting at the window with her hair just gently moving in the breeze, with a blue dress on. And that was it. I never looked at anyone else from there onwards.

The couple returned to New Zealand in 1958 and Peter went back to work for Adrian Timewell. He continued as a watchmaker until he sold his business in Papatoetoe in 1987.

Do you think being in the Air Force changed you?
I think most definitely. At 17, going in, it's very hard to know what I could have done. There was nothing really negative in my service whatsoever. I suppose my age had a lot to do with it. It was an adventure. I often thought I wouldn't have changed how things went. There was never a moment when I hated what I was doing or felt unhappy with life. I've been so lucky in that respect.

'SO THE NAVY IT WAS'

Derek LAVER, 8907,
Able Seaman, RNZN

Derek Laver, the only son of Elsie and Noel Laver, was born in Christchurch in 1925 and grew up in the city, attending Cashmere School and Christchurch Boys' High. Derek vividly recalls the comments of his headmaster at Cashmere School, particularly in the light of his war service in the Navy.

JUST BEFORE WE LEFT, he interviewed each pupil and asked what our ambitions were. I said I was going into the Navy, and he said, 'That's not an ambition. What else do you want to do?' I said, 'I'm going into the Navy.' So he marked my form with 'no ambition'. The next bloke who came up said, 'I'm going to go to sea.' He said, 'You're the same as Laver, you've got no ambition', and he got the same report. I ended up in the Navy and he ended up in the Merchant Navy.

What made you say that you were going to go into the Navy?
I always had a sort of affinity with the sea. I was taken yachting when I was at primary school. A family friend had a 35-foot keeler. We used to do a lot of sailing with him, and I loved it.

Previous page: *Fairmiles on exercises, 1943.* ATL, F-123692-1/2
Above: *Derek Laver, 1944.* Derek Laver collection
Right: *Aerial view of central Christchurch, 1940.* ATL, New Zealand Free Lance Collection, PAColl-8602-38

New Zealand troops in Crete, May 1941. ATL, War History Collection, DA-001157

Derek did not enjoy secondary school and left when he turned 15 in 1940. He remembers that
people were interested in and well informed about the progress of the war.

I think we were pretty aware of what was happening.

Was there much on the radio or in the papers?
It was full of it, especially all the casualties coming through. They were sad days. I can remember at
home when the telegram arrived that my sister's fiancé was missing in action, then some time later that
he was a prisoner of war. There was depths of depression all round the house. A cousin of mine whose
mother used to live with us was also captured. One in Greece and one in Crete. It was a bad time, but
they both got home again.

I'll never forget the day of Pearl Harbor. I know exactly where I was and what I was doing. I had a
little old motorbike in those days. I used to get one gallon of petrol a month with my petrol ration. I'd

just pulled into the service station in Beckenham to cash my one coupon and it came over the radio in the service station that they'd bombed Pearl Harbor. It was an absolute, complete shock.

Did you realise what it would mean?
Not really. I think I took a day or two to realise it. I don't think Japan came much into people's thinking before the war.

How old were you when you thought about joining the Navy?
Eighteen. I wanted to get involved in the war. Everybody thought they should. I didn't fancy the Army or the Air Force, so the Navy it was. With no regrets. I went into the recruiting office and signed the forms. I think I had to get parental permission as well. Funnily, the night before I left, I remember my mother doing the ironing — my last lot of clean clothes to take away. The last thing I saw her ironing was my handkerchiefs. Why that should stick in my mind, I'm damned if I know, but it did.

Derek was told to report to HMNZS Philomel *in Auckland, and was then sent to* HMNZS Tamaki *on Motuihe Island in the Hauraki Gulf for training. It was 1944.*

We went straight out to *Tamaki*. It was up the hill, quite a walk managing a hammock over one shoulder and a kitbag. There were 26 in a class, I think, and there were several classes there at the same time. The first thing was being shown to our barracks, shown how to sling a hammock, and then being told to go to bed. We lay there, terrified to move. After a while you got used to it, but

4-inch naval gun at HMNZS Tamaki. Royal New Zealand Navy Museum, ABZ0191

the first couple of nights I lay there rigidly, sure I was going to fall out, but I never did. We had one blanket and a pillow. There was a bar above the hammock you grabbed with two hands and swung yourself out. They were about six feet or eight feet above the ground.

We did a lot of physical training, gunnery training, tying knots — how to tie and how not to tie — how to read a compass. All the usual requirements of being a seaman. We had gunnery drill with, I don't know what size gun it would be . . . three- or four-inch. All with dummy projectiles. We had to fire 20 rounds with a .303 and 20 with a .22, and I never hit the target once. My hand–eye co-ordination was not good in those days.

The discipline was pretty rugged. You soon got used to it. One of the silliest things I did, I got punished for making a very crude remark during physical training, and the petty officer in charge told me to report to the sick bay and tell them what I'd said. Which I did. I was given a cup of castor oil to drink, to wash my mouth out, and being a brash smart-arse, when I drank it, I

Whaleboat at HMNZS Tamaki.
Royal New Zealand Navy Museum, ABZ0064

said, 'I quite enjoyed that.' They said, 'Good. Have another one.' So I paid.

What other sorts of punishment were there?

You had to run round the parade ground holding what they call a 'projectile', which was the end of a shell. The other one, which I also had inflicted on me involved water. We always had to be conscious of the quantity of fresh water in the reservoirs which were way up the hill, about a 10-minute run. I forget what it was for, but the gunnery officer gave me a cup, and said, 'Run up to the reservoir and fill up that cup. Wave' — because you could see the reservoir — 'and bring the water back because I'm thirsty.' Which I did. He looked at it and said, 'Not thirsty now. Take it back.' That was quite a tough punishment, to run all that way and back in the heat of the summer.

Did you mind those punishments?

No. You earnt it. What you did wrong, you had to get punished for. I wasn't the only bad boy in the group.

Tamaki was an ideal place to train. Lovely beach, and in the summer it was great. Plenty of swimming. We also had to learn how to row. There were whaleboats and cutters, big 32-footers. They took some rowing. The whaleboats were 16 to 20 feet long. On the cutters there were about 16 of us, 8 on each side. I know when I first rowed them, the oars seemed a million miles long. My hands would be shaking away, trying to hold them. The physical training was pretty tough. We were very, very fit when we left there.

Then we went back to *Philomel*, waiting for what was in store for us. That's when I volunteered to go to the naval electrical school to study asdics. I went from there down to Wellington and to the naval electrical school in Petone.

What made you think that you might like to do that?

It appealed to me, I don't know why. Most of them got posted to ships, some of them went into torpedo trainers and depth-charge. Some went on courses, some went to gunneries. There were signalmen as well, telegraphists. We all went different ways.

> *Asdic, later known as sonar, was a secret device for locating submerged submarines by using sound waves. Named after the Anti-Submarine Detection Investigation Committee, it consisted of an electronic sound transmitter and receiver.*

There's a dome on the bottom of the ship that sends a signal out. It goes *ping, ping, ping, ping*. If it locates a submarine, or whatever it may be, you get another *ping* back again. Then you zigzag your ship so when you run out of return pings you know you've passed the stern or the bow, and then you swing back the other way. When you're on duty, you've got headphones on. You do two-hour shifts, and you've got *ping, ping, ping* in your ears — but you get used to it.

What did you do at the training school?

You learnt the basic operation of asdics, how they worked, because when you were on sole charge you had to look after the equipment as well. There was a table with a clear top and you were in another room with your asdic gear on, and there was a silhouette of a submarine and a silhouette of your own ship. You had to pick it up and manoeuvre it and decide whether or not to drop the depth-charges. It was a fun thing, I enjoyed it, almost like kids' PlayStation games. I think in my group there'd be about 10 or 12 of us, and from there they decided what ships we were going to.

Derek returned to Philomel briefly before being posted to a harbour defence motor launch, or HDML, based in Wellington. He had seen a couple of the launches while training at Tamaki.

To me, they looked the most lethal, fast thing you'd ever seen, but they weren't. I went down to Wellington and joined the *1188*. It had a call sign, 'Boldness', but we always had just our fleet number. We weren't important enough to get a name.

What were they designed to do?
Harbour defence was their principal job. If any submarines lurked round the New Zealand coast, we were there to bop them on the head with depth-charges. I think they've proved there were at least a couple of Japanese subs here at one stage, and certainly one German one because they got the logbook. It's been said that the Germans rowed ashore at night and

Harbour defence motor launch Q1188 *travelling at speed on Wellington harbour.*
Derek Laver collection

wandered around on the beach, then they came down and went right past the Wellington Heads. We had a few scares. I remember one particular day when I was at the movies and it came on the screen: 'All naval personnel report back' — so we tore back down and rushed out through the heads to Cook Strait. We never found them.

There were three launches based in Wellington and three in Auckland. They were 72 feet long.

They were not very big. Up for'ard where the crew slept, there were six of us. We had two sets of bunks that folded down during the day to make seats, and another two further aft. On top of that was the wheelhouse, and beyond that the bridge. Down below was a little cabin for the coxswain and the chief motor mechanic, and behind that there was a much bigger cabin for the two officers. Ten men on board. You had to get on pretty well.

We had one bloke who didn't see the necessity for keeping clean. We used to hold him down and take his socks off and make him wash them. God, they used to stink, which is not much fun when you're in close quarters. But, in the main, most of my shipmates were good guys.

Was it pretty much the same crew the whole time?
We had a change of seaman once, and telegraphist once in the 12 months.

Shelly Bay was what they call our home port, we operated from there. We used to go on patrol at Worser Bay. There would be two HDs at a time moored to a mooring, which in southerly storms wasn't much fun. Right across the Wellington Heads there was a cable. As each ship went over it, it sent a signal back to the lookout point, and if it wasn't expected then we would be advised to investigate, which only happened once when we were tied up there. We got this message that something was coming and it shouldn't be there, so we up-anchored and went chasing this damn thing, and eventually caught up with it. I got it on the asdic beam because it was pretty foggy. The fog lifted and we could see it was the old *Echo* scow from Picton. He forgot to get a clearance. I believe he got quite a roasting over it.

If it had been an enemy ship, what would you have done?
If it had been a submarine, we'd have dropped depth-charges on it. If it had been an enemy ship, I don't know what the hell we'd have done with our piddly little guns. We had an Oerlikon, which is about 78-millimetre, and a Browning twin machine gun. Eight depth-charges, and the officers had revolvers.

Five days we'd do out there, and back into port for three. Say we went out Monday to Friday, there'd be one there when we got there. It'd go back to port, then after three days there'd be another change, so there weren't the same two there at the same time. On the way out we used to practise on the *South Sea*, a little minesweeper which was sunk — it hit the *Wahine* earlier in the war. Some nights we'd practise on the inter-island ferry. The skipper thought I was doing it visually, not by sound, so he blacked the windows out. He got excited and forgot what we were doing. At the last minute he

Shelly Bay naval base. Royal New Zealand Navy Museum, ACE0009

screamed, 'Hard aport!' I spun the wheel and we missed the ferry by bloody inches, it seemed. It was the last time we did it that way.

The four seamen used to do cooking a fortnight each. A lot of us had never cooked before. We had a young bloke, every day he'd go to the coxswain: how do you want this cooked? How do you want that cooked? How do you want the cabbage cooked? Every day it was: put it in a saucepan, cover it with water, put some salt in it, bring it to the boil. After about 10 days the coxswain got very upset. He said, 'Fry the effing stuff!' I went down below and went into the galley. He had a great big frying pan, full of fat, with cabbage leaves in it. We had some very ropy meals. We had fellas, they'd roast corned beef, and serve pork thinking it was lamb. On one occasion, I was duty cook and a bloke walked down

An off-duty rating aboard a harbour defence motor launch.
ATL, John Pascoe Collection, F-922-1/4

through the mess deck who'd just been transferred to our ship. He said, 'What time do you eat on this thing?' I said, 'Midday.' He said, 'It'd better be a big feed. I'm a farmer's boy and I eat big.' I said, 'We're having a roast, so you'll be well fed.' I served the meal, put it out. There was no sign of this bloke. I said, 'Has anyone seen that new fella?' They said, 'What new fella?' I said, 'He's just joined the ship.' I went up on deck and he's sitting on the wharf, his head between his hands, being violently seasick. There wasn't a ripple on the water.

How did you wash on board the ship?

There was a kerosene tin. We cut the side out of it, not the top, and then filled that with hot water. You sat with your backside in the water and your feet hanging over the end, and washed yourself as best you could. Then you'd stand up and wash the rest, then pick it up and tip it over your head. We did our washing the same way. When we got into barracks, of course, it was all hands to the showers.

Where were your action stations?

On the wheel on my asdic gear. When there were action stations, originally they'd just give a blast of the hooter, and you'd all report to the bridge to be advised what type of action was to take place. I remember we were coming out of Wellington, getting out towards the heads, and it was as rough as buggery, and the alarm went. Our stoker used to man the for'ard Browning gun. He thought he'd be a smart-arse and show how efficient he was, so he went straight up from the engine room and tore down the port side of the ship, just as we took a big wave over. Knocked him flat on his back. He stormed back to bridge and said, 'What sort of a bloody fool would have gunnery practice on a day like this?' 'Actually the HDML astern of us is on fire. Get those hoses coupled.' We got alongside this thing, but the fire was out when we got there. From that day on, we had different signals. One for fire; one for gunnery; one for depth-charges.

Did you get a rum ration?

Yes, if you wanted it. You either had your rum ration, or threepence a day in lieu. I took a rum ration. We used to test it periodically because we had an idea our coxswain was watering it down, but we never caught him. We'd pour a little bit of it on the deck, and put a match to it. If it spluttered, it had water in it. The big thing was to try and smuggle it into a bottle and take it ashore, which we did a few times.

Did you have those things like sippers and gulpers?

If I had my rum ration, I'd tell you and say, 'Sippers.' You'd take a sip. 'Gulpers', you'd take a mouthful, and 'Scupper', you tossed the lot back. There'd be a big fanny that held it all — a fanny's like a big saucepan — then they had a little measurement to pull it out and pour it into a glass. Ration was at 11 o'clock. The expression was, 'Up spirits. Stand by the Holy Ghost.' 'Up spirits' was when you drank it. I don't know why the 'Stand by the Holy Ghost' came into it.

When you were moored to the buoy at Worser Bay, what sort of things did you do to pass the time when you weren't on watch?

Wash the decks, dry the decks. Wash the decks, dry the decks! We used to play cards, a lot of '500' and euchre. There was a piece in one of the Auckland papers just after the war about our fleet, saying it was probably the loneliest, most boring job in the whole New Zealand Navy. They were right.

Did you think that at the time?

No.

Tell me about Navy Week in Nelson.

We did a 'show the flag' cruise to Nelson. The Patriotic Board designated that week as Navy Week to raise funds. We were halfway through Cook Strait and we got a message that there were three unidentified vessels in the strait which could be suspicious, so we started rushing round, asdics going. Then we got another message from Stephens Island that it was us. The naval authorities had forgotten to advise them.

We got to French Pass between D'Urville Island and the mainland, which is a notorious stretch of water because the tide just rushes through like a whirlpool. No ship goes through unless it's slack water,

A post-war photograph of the Maimai *alongside a Wellington wharf.*
ATL, M. Berthold Collection, F-25423-1/4

which is halfway between the tides. Our skipper decided that the Navy didn't wait for time and tide, and went straight through at high water. We spun round like a cork. We got through by the skin of our teeth. Going back, we waited for slack water.

We got to Nelson, tied up, and the first thing that happened, the skipper called us all up — there were three ships, three HDs — lined us up on the wharf and said they wanted volunteers to accompany young ladies on street corners to sell war bonds. Strictly voluntary. Nobody volunteered. He went away and came back an hour later. Formed us up again and said, 'I got it wrong. You don't have to sell war bonds, you've just got to stand and accompany your young lady.' So we all volunteered. I got the youngest, and she'd never see 60 again. When we got there, we were told that Harley's brewery was free to sailors for the day, so we all hightailed it up there. I was the last to get there. They had a special brew that they'd made. God, it was good. I stayed half, three-quarters of an hour, rushed back, found my young lady on the street corner, grabbed a handful of war bonds and marched round the streets. I didn't do too badly either, sold quite a number.

They decided we would do a mock anti-submarine patrol in the inner harbour. We had little 50-pound depth-charges which were launched by hand, but the Patriotic Board was not aware of how these things worked. When you drop a depth-charge, it's the depth of the water that decides where it'll go off. The minimum depth was 50 feet. It was low tide, there was less than 50 feet of water, so our depth-charges hit the bottom before they exploded. All the pressure came upwards, none went down. We lifted our stern right out of the water, broke the toilet in the men's toilet, people on the wharf were terrified, and they told me it broke a lot of the glasses in the wharf pub, which was partly on the wharf. It wasn't a hell of a successful demonstration. That was Navy Week.

Occasionally we'd escort the *Maimai*, which was a 'sweeper, out into Cook Strait and round about. We were classified harbour defence. After the war, when they gave our service medals out, they decided that New Zealand waters were part of the Pacific war zone, so we were given the Pacific Star. You also got a half a crown daily gratuity for going overseas, ninepence a day in New Zealand. Then they decided after the war that those who served in New Zealand waters were entitled to an extra ninepence. I applied for that. We were informed that because we were harbour defence, we weren't entitled to it. We went on a 'show the flag' cruise to Nelson, we went to Christchurch, Timaru, Oamaru, Dunedin, Bluff and back, and from Wellington to Auckland, so we certainly didn't stay inside the heads.

We got some pretty hairy times on those trips. When we left Wellington down to Christchurch, we sailed for two hours, and I don't think I've ever been in a sea like it. The waves were so high that our 70 feet was like a car going uphill, and crashed down the other side. We lost about 30 feet of the rubbing strake, which is big heavy timber between the deck and the side, so we decided we'd have to go back to port. It was too dangerous. I was on the wheel on that occasion. We managed to turn round, and it was like hydro-sliding going back. We were two hours going out, we were back alongside in an hour. Because it was a cross sea, we just missed Barrett Reef on one side and almost went aground on the side of Wellington harbour. It wasn't much fun. Two days later, after we'd been repaired, we sailed again to Lyttelton. It was just like rowing down Colombo Street. Not a ripple on the water.

You played cricket one season.

Yes, mainly in Wellington. The naval area there, which was the minesweeper and the HDs, naval headquarters and the training places, had a team in the Wellington Cricket Association. I thought I wouldn't mind having a go, so Wally Mapplebeck, a Canterbury Plunket Shield player, a nice guy, a lieutenant, he arranged for me to have a net trial, which I did and they said, 'Yes, you're in the team.' Every Saturday I had to have leave. Even when we were at Worser Bay the skipper would have to go and tie up at the wharf at Seatoun and let me ashore. Away I'd go to cricket, come back afterwards on the tram, stand on the end of the wharf and wave. The skipper hated it, but my war stopped. Our skipper was a non-cricket-lover, so Able Seaman Laver was not his favourite.

It was decided that we'd go up to Waiouru — there was a naval establishment at Waiouru — so the cricket team went up there and had a one-day game at Waiouru. Then we came down to Christchurch and played the Christchurch base and the crews of the ships here. We had a three-day game with them. That was good. We played the Army at the Basin Reserve. That was quite a thrill.

After VE Day, they decided they'd swap the two flotillas, so we sailed to Auckland and the Auckland ones came to Wellington. We spent a bit of time on patrol. Until VJ Day we used to patrol round the Hauraki Gulf. We caught fire there one night. That wasn't much fun. One of our blokes had washed his overalls and wanted them for the next day. After we'd all gone to bed he hung them over a rail in the galley and lit the kerosene stove, then went to sleep. We woke up to find that the timber between the galley and the fuel tanks was starting to smoulder. However, we got it out all right. It made a hell of a mess, there was foam all over the shot. Luckily somebody woke up in time to put it out. Another couple of minutes, it could have been a lot worse.

Derek does not have very fond memories of the US troops he came into contact with in Auckland.

I remember I was walking down Queen Street and this big, burly American Marine put his arm around some girl who obviously was protesting. I thought, This bloke's too big for me, so I walked up and said, 'Hello, darling. Sorry I'm late.' She took the bait and said, 'That's all right, dear, I've only just got here.' The Yank said, 'Sorry, buddy. I didn't know it was your girl', and took off. She and I had a lovely night at the movies.

We got involved in a pretty big brawl in Queen Street. The Yanks used to have big, thick leather belts. They used to whip them off and wrap them round their knuckles, which used to inflict a fair bit of damage. The police eventually arrived, and the American patrol car, and everything cleared.

The first time I went to one of the service clubs, there was a notice on the wall: any American serviceman who would like a good home-cooked meal to ring this phone number. One of my mates was a farmer's son from Southland way, virtually never been off the farm until he joined the Navy, and he got quite wound up about it, saying, 'I love food. I love a good home-cooked roast. Why should these bloody Yanks get it and not me?' He was very bitter about the whole thing.

Preparing flags for the VE Day celebrations, Wellington, May 1945.
ATL, John Pascoe Collection, F-1507-1/4

Derek recalls the celebrations in Wellington to mark VE Day, 8 May 1945.

We had our what they call 'splice the mainbrace', which is an extra rum ration, that morning, and then we were let loose on the poor Wellington public. I got arrested. I tried to steal a New Zealand flag off the front of the St George Hotel. I got on top of a car — I was encouraged by a sub-lieutenant who happened to be there as well. Next thing a couple of policemen came along and marched me down the street on the way to the cells. Halfway down the street, a naval patrol arrived, and asked what had happened. They said, 'We'll arrest this bloke.' The police let me off and I was marched though Wellington with a couple of naval police guards. We went down an alleyway and stopped. One pulled a bottle of beer out of his jacket, said, 'Have a beer, sailor, and for Christ's sake, behave yourself', and they walked away and left me. It was good, but it was nothing like VJ Day. That was much more exuberant, I think, a real wild and woolly night in Auckland. The whole of Queen Street seemed to be full of people dancing, singing and carrying on.

When it was all over, they decommissioned all the ships and took them up to Pine Island, which is now I think called Herald Island. Our HD was the escort. We used to tow the Fairmiles up there after getting their tanks steam-dried. All the minesweepers were brought up there, and the HDs, and I was sent up there as a watch-keeper until I got discharged. Or almost. Our *1188* looked the saddest of the lot of them. All the happy times I'd had on it.

Harbour defence motor launch Q1189 *on patrol, 1943.* ATL, John Pascoe Collection, F-914-1/4

Tell me what the Fairmiles were.

They were like an enlarged HD. They were built in New Zealand, 120 feet long. They served up in the Islands, on anti-submarine patrols and general duties.

Then I was sent back to *Philomel*, waiting for my final discharge. I had a crazy job back there while I was waiting. On the wharf where the *Philomel* was tied up, they had the stores for the outstations like *Tamaki* and Great Barrier Island. Most of them were closed so there was no need for a *Tamaki* storeman, but the Navy still had one — me. I had a little office on the wharf, and a sort of a sofa thing which I could sleep on if I wanted to. I used to read and write letters and doze. I worked from eight till four, or at least I had to be there till four, then I was free till eight the next morning. When I got my discharge in August 1946, I was replaced. There might still be someone on that wharf acting as *Tamaki* storeman.

Derek returned to office work in Christchurch. He met his first wife, Aileen, in 1947 and they married in 1948. They had two children, Phillipa and John. In 1970, the couple separated and Derek married Janice in 1974. Derek retired as the managing editor of Christchurch Community Newspapers in 1985.

I'd meet people afterwards who would say, 'What did you do?' I'd tell them and they'd say, 'You weren't really in the war, were you?' It hurt like hell, because every man-jack of us felt the same — we would have loved to have gone overseas. It wasn't our choice.

Do you belong to the RSA?

No. Although we were entitled to join, I was so sensitive at that stage about not having been overseas. I did join it for a little while, but I thought, No, I don't belong here. I thought it was for people who'd served, actually fought. A lot of guys went overseas and never saw a bullet fired, but you're a bit bolshie in your thinking when you're 20 or 21.

I have no regrets, I enjoyed it. When you think back on it, the whole damn thing's illogical. Why we can't get on and live together peacefully, I'll never know. When you're young, it's a great adventure. When you're old and look back on it, you think, How bloody stupid.

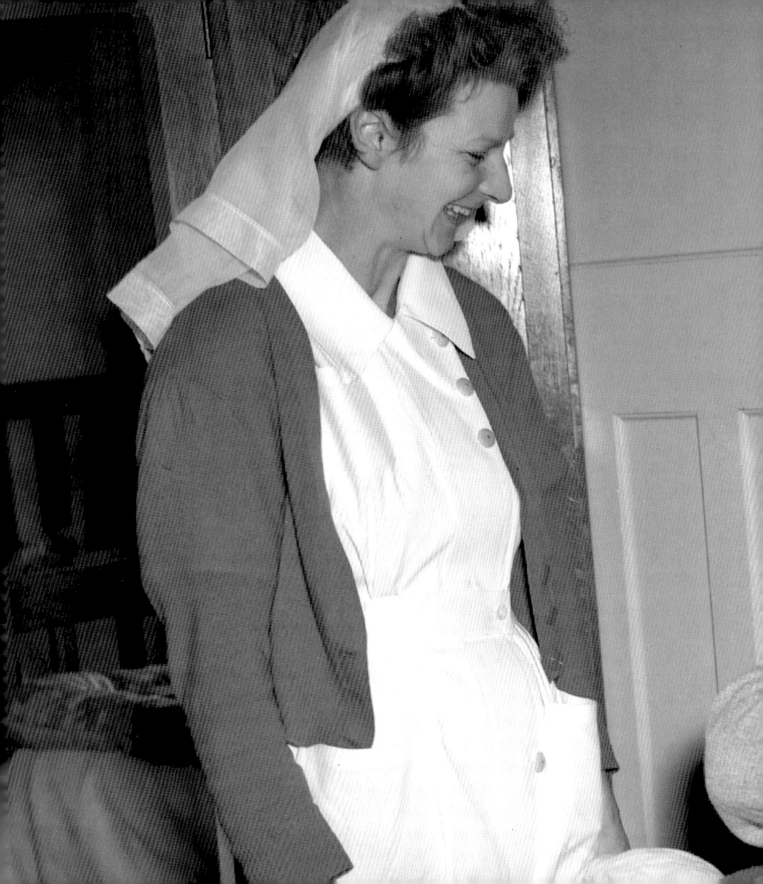

'ORDINARY
NURSING DUTIES'

Maisie TAKLE, W4470, Corporal, WAAF

As a child, Maisie Younger moved with her family to Auckland from Taumarunui, where she had been born in 1920, to live in the suburb of Mt Eden. Her father Jack was a fruiterer in Dominion Road, and her mother Florence worked at home. Maisie attended Mt Eden School and then Kowhai Junior High before leaving at the age of 13. It was the middle of the Depression and jobs were scarce.

I WENT TO WORK AT 13. I'd never been out on my own much at all, and it was a shock, but I managed. The school of life, really. I worked at Farmers' Trading Company. I went into the sewing department. I worked there quite a while doing messages and ordinary little things, then they put me on a machine. I loved it, but they came along the next day, and said, 'Sorry, we'll have to take you off. You're not old enough to work on a machine.' So I was demoted, and had to wait till I was older — I think it must have been 15, I'm not sure, but I know I was disgusted.

What were they sewing?
Everything. It was a huge place. There was a tailoring section, which I eventually got into, and I liked that. They did tents and sheets. There was whirr and noise. I'd never seen anything like it. Then I went off to another place and ended up making dresses for a warehouse in Elliott Street.

The Farmers' Trading Company, Hobson Street, Auckland, 1924.
Special Collections, Auckland City Libraries, 1-W302

Previous page: *An Air Force nurse talking to a patient.* RNZAF Official, via Air Force Museum, Christchurch, PR3843
Above: *Maisie Takle.* Maisie Takle collection

Can you remember hearing that war had been declared?

Yes, yes. My mother's two brothers had been in the First World War and I'd heard all the dreadful part, and I always prayed that I'd never have to be in that situation, but it did come. It was a big worry. I don't know if the boys thought it was a good idea or what, but they were all enlisting — my three brothers and Ken, who was my fiancé by that time, and his twin brother, and cousins. It was a big exodus in our lives. It was a worrying time.

> *Maisie had met her fiancé, Kennedy Takle, through mutual friends.*

He was a very nice boy, we got on very well, always did. He had to be someone my brothers liked, that was my criteria. And he was. He mixed in well with them all.

Did he talk to you about enlisting?

He didn't want to go away at all. He was a home boy, he really was, but I think there was no other thing to do. He just had to do it, it was his duty. I don't think the boys of today would be so willing to go. I hope they don't. I hope they never have to do it.

> *Ken trained at Papakura camp, before going to Te Rapa, near Hamilton. He had three lots of final leave before he was sent to the Middle East.*

How did you feel when he left to go overseas?

You just had to get on with it. We got married before he went, in February 1940. My brothers had gone, and I just accepted it. I had to. And because my brothers were all in the forces, and he was, and cousins, I wasn't going to be left home not doing something, so I joined the Red Cross and did all the exams. You had to do 60 hours in a hospital to get your VAD certificate, and I did that at the Auckland Hospital and then was posted to the Ellerslie racecourse.

> *The study for the Red Cross exams was all done out of work hours.*

It did take a while by the time you got through the different certificates, but it was worthwhile.

Maisie Takle (front, fourth from right) with other VADs at the military annexe of Auckland Hospital, Ellerslie racecourse. Maisie Takle collection

What made you choose nursing?

I always wanted to be a nurse, but you had to pay a training fee in those days and my parents just couldn't afford it, and I couldn't.

When you went to Ellerslie, was that full-time?

Yes. Ellerslie was the military annexe attached to the Auckland Hospital, in the big old building behind the stands. The dining room, stewards' room, all the rooms were used by the hospital. It was strange. There were beds everywhere, even in the tote at one stage, and in the bar. I'd never been in a bar in my life, but I was in the bar scrubbing the bar top.

Who were you looking after?

They were mainly Army boys. Some Air Force, and very few Navy, because they had their own hospital. They were boys who couldn't be sent home, but they couldn't be left in camp. There were flu and related types of illnesses that weren't serious. Retired nursing sisters came in and took over the wards, and we were their nurses. They kept training us. It was very good. Strict, my word they were strict. You had to mitre the corners of the beds, and you didn't run unless it was haemorrhage or fire, which we never had. I was eager and was always almost running around, and I was told many times not to run. Not haemorrhage or fire! Sister White was the one I remember most. She'd been a missionary up in the Islands, the Solomons I think it was.

What sort of uniform did you have?

We had a creamy white smock — it was probably unbleached calico — which they supplied, with a drawstring waist, and we wore our Red Cross veils. The St John people had their St John caps. We all got on very well. There were lots of patients and they came and went. The flu took over for a while and they had to have more wards opening. We had two or three doctors who came in every day. There was quite a big staff.

Maisie in her Red Cross VAD uniform. Maisie Takle collection

Those Red Cross veils were flimsy. They were organdie, very soft. One day my veil just took off with the wind. It went swirling up into the air and ended up on the flagstaff. One of the orderlies got up and brought it down. We all thought it was a great joke, but matron didn't. She was very disgusted.

Maisie enjoyed the fact that the annexe was at the racecourse.

They were still exercising the horses. We'd see the horses being walked around. It was great.

Did they have race meetings?

Yes, we had several while I was there. The boys who would have gone home on a Friday would all think, Oh, races, and they'd get much sicker on the Friday when the doctor came round so they could stay. They were allowed to go out at the top of the grandstand to watch the races, but they had to wear their pyjamas and a very awful grey dressing gown so they'd be known. They weren't allowed to wander, but they enjoyed it.

Maisie worked at the Ellerslie annexe for around nine months until demand for Red Cross helpers dropped off.

They said we would have to go to the meatworks, which was a horrifying thought, or nurse at the Greenlane old people's part, or continue training, or join the forces. I opted to join the Air Force. I was sorry I didn't do my training, but I thought at that time that the war would be well over before three or four years' training was done.

It was 1941. Maisie went to the drill hall in Rutland Street for her interview and medical, and was accepted. She was sent to Rotorua for three weeks, and then down to Rongotai.

I had never been away on my own before. We had to be taken to the railway station to catch the *Herald* train that went through to Rotorua. There were several other girls there, waiting to go. The stationmaster locked us in the waiting room, I couldn't imagine what for. He said, 'There'll be a lot of naval and that sort of people around soon. I'll wake you up when it's time for the train to go. Don't worry.' I don't think any of us slept, but I often thought he was a kind man.

What made you choose the Air Force?
Ken was in the Army and my two brothers were in the Air Force, and I thought I'd prefer the Air Force. They didn't like married couples being together, so I could never go away on a hospital ship because they wouldn't let you.

I'd been told dreadful tales about going into barracks, and I didn't know what was going to happen. When I arrived, we were sent to a private hotel because the Air Force had taken over all these private hotels in Rotorua, so we were very well treated. We were waited on, I couldn't believe it. We had damask cloths on the table. I was only there three weeks and then I went to Rongotai, which again was different because the WAAF barracks hadn't been built and I had to go to a bed-and-breakfast up the

New Zealand Centennial Exhibition buildings, 1940. ATL, Evening Post Collection, G-48873-1/4

road somewhere. I had to find my own way round and I didn't know Wellington at all. I was in a state of shock for quite a while.

Rongotai airbase used many of the buildings that had been built for the 1940 Centennial Exhibition. Maisie and her brother had been to the Exhibition.

The whole Exhibition was great. When I got there, the Air Force had taken it over — and the round dining room had become part of the hospital.

I went straight onto duties. We did three shifts. Most of the girls lived off-station because they were Wellington dwellers. We had wards, and the orderlies mainly worked the nights because the WAAFs weren't on-station. All the daily sick parades were down at the end of the hospital. We only went down there at certain times; mainly we did the wards. There were boys from the Islands coming back with malaria and that type of thing as well. Anything serious went to Wellington Hospital.

We were just erks to start with — that was our name for ratings — and then we did lectures and exams through our hospital, and I became a corporal at one stage, which was most unusual. I was among the first ones who got to be a corporal, and that wasn't till I went up to Hobsonville. It was quite a while before they decided the girls could have ranks. This was because the Red Cross was non-combatant.

What was the nurse's uniform like?
It was very nice, silky. The officers had a lovely shirt — a more silky material than the ordinary Air Force boys — and it was made of that material, Air Force blue. We still wore our veils and floated round the campus. They were tied at the back but the wind floated them up a bit. You had plenty of hairclips. We wore white stockings.

Once the WAAF accommodation was built, Maisie lived on-station at Rongotai.

They were new prefabricated type of things. I was in a room with about 10 girls at that stage. We had to get up in the morning and make our [blanket] pack. I always thought what a waste of time it was, but they had inspections every so many days, so you never quite knew when you had to have your pack made. If you'd been working till 10 o'clock that night, from 3 till 10, you had to still get up and have your pack done, which was quite a nuisance.

What was it like living in a room with so many other girls?
I quite enjoyed it. It was company. They were all good sports. They'd come from all over New Zealand.

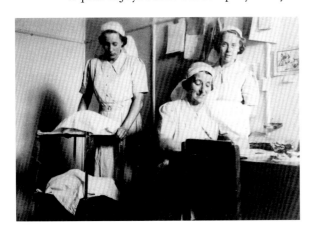

None of the other nurses at that stage lived on-station.

Did any of them get homesick and want to go home?
I don't think so. There was always something going on.

Maisie (right) in the duty room at Rongotai airbase.
Maisie Takle collection

Lighting the gas fire and making toast by it at night, that sort of thing. It was good fun. They were all good company.

Strangely enough, people took for granted that they were naughty girls, and they weren't. I knew of someone who had an incomplete abortion. That was frightening. I had [to deal with] that on my own one night. I didn't know what it was, I was too naïve and young. I tried to ring the doctor, and he was busy. In the finish I got hold of the ambulance and we took the girl up to the hospital. I learnt next morning that that's what it had been. They were a well-behaved lot.

Maisie describes her ward duties.

I'd say our role would be equivalent to a nurse aide now. You made beds, gave sponge baths, gave out medicines, made sure patients didn't walk out when they shouldn't — ordinary nursing duties. The sister was there if you needed her in the day, but not at night for quite a long time, which was a nuisance. The doctor would come and do his rounds.

We had a marvellous system. If anyone had something wrong and you didn't know what it was, they were sent to 'sick and wounded'. You filled in a form and they went to 'sick and wounded' and you never saw them again.

We had about one day a week off, I think. It was no hardship because there was nothing to do. We'd go to a film with a group — we always went out in a group — and walk home round the waterfront, round Oriental Bay, which was very pleasant. We'd get a trip to Auckland, and we were allowed to go home for a week or two, with our ration cards. We didn't have to have ration cards, but when you went home on leave you got the ration cards to take with you, which people were grateful for. I think they were for tea, sugar, butter. And clothing coupons.

I don't think I was ever asked to do drill. They had to parade for their pay — pay parade — but I never went on one. We'd just ring up and say, 'Can we come over now, while we're not busy?' At Hobsonville it was different. We'd hire the ambulance and go up and get our pay. I was the only nurse there for a long time, and the doctor and I would go up and get our pay when there was no flying going on. The ambulance had to stay at the station while the flying was going on. I think I went on one parade before I came out. I wanted to know what they did. They just stood there, and marched, and stood again, and marched. It wasn't very interesting, I was glad I never did it. They did exercise programmes at Hobsonville, but I never had to go on those. I'd stay on duty at the section. If anybody wanted things after certain hours, there had to be somebody there, so I didn't really have to do marching and things like that.

The Air Force band was quite famous. Was it stationed at Rongotai?
At different times they were based at Rongotai, and other times at different stations through New

US troops on a troop train at Wellington, 1942. ATL, War History Collection, F-32265-1/4

WAAF medical orderly with a patient at Whenuapai, 1942. RNZAF Official, via Air Force Museum, Christchurch, PR80a

Zealand. They did their marching practice and things. They marched with the American band after the Manners Street fights.

Maisie recalls her own involvement with the aftermath of the Manners Street brawl in Wellington in 1943 between NZ and US troops.

I was off duty. We'd been out at the pictures and when we came home, a terrible lot of Air Force boys were in the corridor being treated for, I think, injuries to eyes and teeth and noses. Minor things. The next morning all the beds were full of these boys who'd had a fight with the Americans. I never did find out what it was all about. We were busy treating the sick and wounded.

They brought the bands in. An American big band was in Wellington at the time, and they brought the two bands together at Rongotai, and both bands played and marched together. And they had a big — was it a meal? I can't remember the meal part, but we did something and they all mixed together, and I think peace was restored. It was a while before the Americans were allowed leave in Wellington.

There was a feeling that the Americans were show-offs. They did have lovely uniforms, I believe. Our Air Force boys weren't so badly off, but the Army boys had ordinary, rough sort of uniforms. There was a feeling that any of our girls who went out with the American boys were no good, no good at all. None of us ever went out with an American. We wouldn't dare. We didn't want to.

Apart from the patients, did you have much to do with the men in the Air Force?
Not really. They used to have section dances at Hobsonville and Rongotai. Each section would be in charge of arranging that night, and they'd have girls come in from the town. Busloads would come and dance. That was about the only time that we mixed with them. We had . . . almost a family. We all knew each other and were like brothers and sisters. They were good company. We weren't allowed to wear our wedding ring on duty, or our engagement rings. They had to go round our neck on a chain, hidden, because it wasn't hygienic. They were very strict as far as nursing procedures were concerned. I'd go over to the dance, and the boys would say my ring was a protection ring. They didn't believe I was married. They sang 'Mairzy Doats' to me. Awful. Awful. I hate that song.

Were they good to you, the men?
Yes, they were like big brothers. I'd been brought up with three older brothers and we used to do everything together, and it was just a continuation of that. Some of them were a bit older, the rest were young boys who were training. They were just like family.

Did you have to salute officers?
Not unless you were in uniform, and I never was. The officers in Rongotai saluted the veil, you'd say. It was a mark of respect, and we didn't have to salute back because we weren't in uniform. The only lady Air Force officer that we had was a doctor. The others were Army nursing sisters.

Were there men in there who had VD?

It wasn't spoken about much at all. When I was at Hobsonville I came into touch with it more, being the only nurse there. The doctor would ask for a special tray, and I knew what that was for. The tray was taken into his office, and he did it all.

We had a special clinic at Hobsonville called the blue light. If the boys had been in town and been playing up or been with someone they didn't know very well, if they used that equipment — it was syringes and different things — they didn't have to use their names. They had to put a sign on one part of a paper, and took the other half with them, and the date, and they didn't lose their pay if they had any disease. If they hadn't used that blue light and they did get something wrong, they lost their pay. We didn't come into contact with it a lot, but we knew it was there. It was only after I'd been given my corporal's stripes that I was allowed to go and look after that part, which meant taking things out, sterilising them and putting back fresh things.

What was Rongotai station for?

It was a training station. They had courses for electricians, and stores, and that sort of thing. The boys used to come in quite a big influx and do these courses, then they'd go back to their own stations, so it was a moving population. Hobsonville was more settled.

How did you get transferred up to Hobsonville?

I asked to go up on compassionate leave because my brother had been badly wounded in the Middle East and was on the very sick list. He had a very bad stomach wound. He'd been given up by our boys. He said he could remember they walked past and said, 'Don't pick him up, his stomach's gone.' The Tommies came along, stretcher-bearers, and picked him up and took him to their hospital. The doctor there saved his life, but he was on the very ill list for a long, long time and my poor mother was in Auckland on her own, more or less, and with all this going on, I thought it was time I went home.

Maisie worked for around two years at the clinic at Hobsonville, where the men would attend their sick parades.

There was one early morning, at seven o'clock, and then there was one at lunchtime, and one in the

Kennedy Takle.
Maisie Takle collection

afternoon. There was a doctor there every day, and orderlies. We never had patients there, only outpatients. There was a bed there in one of the rooms, but we never used it for the patients. 'Specials' came down for injections, but they didn't need bed care.

We had VJ Day while I was there, a big celebration on station. When we heard the war was over, we whooped around the station. We got in the ambulance, and the fire brigade was down there somehow, and we whooped around the station with all the bells and the sirens blowing. It was fun. The boys went up to the canteen, and I went on the ambulance. That really was a celebration, because we knew then that our time was coming, that we could finish. I've seen photographs of them parading up in town, but we didn't do that. It was wonderful, it really was. We couldn't believe it after all that time. We were very fortunate because it was only my one brother who was wounded, and he came home on a hospital ship. We were very fortunate as a family that we didn't have those immediate bereavements like some did.

What was it like for you, thinking about your husband coming home?
It was just over four years [we'd been apart]. It was a long, long time and I felt I'd grown up in that time. It did feel strange, and I didn't know how it was going to work out because, I mean, we'd been marvellous friends and mates and all that, but it was a big process being away all that time from each other. I was quite disturbed, wondering how it would work out. Fortunately, it was good. It was wonderful. He came and it was all right again. It was my Ken back again, and that was wonderful. But it was a nervous time, wondering.

Were you able to meet him?
Yes, at the railway station in Auckland. All the family went, my mother and father, my mother-in-law, and they were all looking at us. We both looked at each other, and oh, it was scary and it was wonderful. I remember his mother kept saying, 'Kiss her. Kiss her. Kiss her.' All we wanted to do was look at each other, and hug. We didn't want to kiss at that stage. It was good. Really, I was very fortunate. We had

a marvellous marriage and two wonderful children, and grandchildren and great-grandchildren now. I was very lucky.

I didn't know at the time, but he was feeling the same as I was. How is this going to work out? But it was all right. We were just a couple of older kids than we'd been when we started.

He didn't let on, but he'd been playing rugby for the Army over in Egypt somewhere, and he'd had his top front teeth kicked out. He had to go to hospital and they gave him a plate which he apparently didn't want to wear and wouldn't wear until he got news he was coming home. His mates — by this time they'd all been together for a long time — wouldn't let him eat until he'd put his teeth in. They said, 'You're not going home to Maisie without those teeth. You've got to wear them.' They kept at him until he did.

We went to live with his father and looked after him for 23 years.

Ken returned to work at the family firm, Takle Brothers, who dealt in upholsterers' supplies. Maisie quickly became pregnant and did not work outside the home after the couple's first child was born. In 1981, Ken Takle died. Maisie, who still lives in Auckland, reflects on her time in the Air Force.

It was a good life. I wouldn't want to do it again, but at the time it was a marvellous fill-in for those years that Ken was away. Some girls were left with children to bring up, and that must have been very hard because the children wouldn't know their dads when they came back. I matured and learnt loyalty and friendship. I did feel it was good for me.

'IRONING THE BILLIARD TABLE'

Heather CRISPE, W441, Ordinary Wren, WRNZNS

Heather Jerram, the daughter of Les and Vera Jerram, was born in Auckland in 1924. After service in the First World War, Les Jerram trained as a surveyor and eventually went to work for the British government in what was then Malaya. His family joined him, but later Heather and her elder sister Claire returned to New Zealand to attend secondary school.

THE WAR CAME and my mother was sent down from Malaya because my father felt that it was likely to be devastating with the Japs coming into the war. He was caught up in it. He'd been seconded into the Army and took the rank of captain. He was caught in Singapore and dispatched in a cattle truck — four days, four nights — up to Siam, to those camps that we've all read about, such as Kanburi and the River Kwai.

Mother and I and my sister were very upset about this, because we didn't hear from him at all. Being a good, conscientious person I decided I had to do something, so I put my name down for the Navy, and I was accepted.

What made you choose the Navy?
I have no idea. I think the uniform, probably. Going out to Westfield, packing meat, was the other alternative if you didn't go into the forces. You'd be manpowered.

Heather enlisted in 1943 and was posted to Devonport naval base.

Previous page: *Heather Crispe's 'showman' number in the Wrens' show.* Peter and Heather Crispe collection
Above: *Heather Jerram.* Peter and Heather Crispe collection

Manpowered women working at a vegetable dehydration plant in Pukekohe. ATL, John Pascoe Collection, C-923-1/2

I got my papers, and then we had to have a full medical. There were several of us, about eight, I think, going in that day for the medical. It was all so exciting. I met a lovely girl called Pam Murray and we became such friends. She was lucky, she got a job on the shore as a driver, because she could drive a car. She drove all the officers around Auckland. We all went up to the Auckland Hospital and had X-rays and examinations. It was pretty cursory. We were all 100 per cent fit and got our admission papers, I suppose, soon after that, and that's when I went into the Navy.

They gave us wonderful uniforms. We got two big topcoats. One was a proper gabardine raincoat, and the other one was a thick wool cloth, a beautiful thing. We had slouch hats at that stage with just

Heather Jerram (right) with Esme McLeod at the Auckland central post office.
Peter and Heather Crispe collection

'HMS' on them, no place where we were. Beautiful grey gloves, grey stockings, several pairs of shoes, and a going-out suit made for us and tailored at the Farmers' Trading Company. We got all our shirts and two or three sets of overalls, just a dress type of thing. They had holes in them that we had to laboriously put special naval buttons on. Every time they were washed, we took them off and then we put them all back again. There were lots of them; everything was double-breasted in the Navy. Trousers were not in vogue in those days. We all had skirts. They were fairly long, about mid-calf, and quite firm-fitting. Not a lot of material in them, but they had a slit up the back so you could climb up a companionway without falling over.

When we first went in, we had a week of being told how to drill. We went on route marches and we also had films of the awful things that happened to girls who didn't behave with men. They gave us all the gruesome details of gonorrhoea and syphilis. And very gory details they were. We had to learn all the jargon. We had to learn how to do knots and ropes. That was the first week. Then we were put in our various places, and I thought, Gosh, how am I going to be an officer's steward? I've hardly ever even done the dishes. I had learnt to cook with my grandmother in my school holidays a bit, but I was only a pantry hand so I really didn't need to cook. I just chopped up lettuce very fine — it had to be so fine it was like hair — and tomatoes. We put them in lovely entrée dishes — rows of carrot, rows of tomatoes, cucumber — all most beautifully put out for the officers.

That went on for some time. I had a girl with me in the pantry, Hazel. We were between the cooking staff and all the stewards in the wardroom, and did all the passing of the plates and the washing up.

In time, Heather was promoted to being a steward in the officers' wardroom.

It was for the officers who were either in port on their ships, or working on the dockyard. It was a big dockyard, of course, repairing ships. So there was a big staff, coming and going. There were medical officers too.

In the pantry we wore our navy overalls with all the buttons, but in the wardroom we wore white. They were washed and ironed over in the Auckland laundry, so we didn't have to do them. Our navy blue overalls we wore when we were cleaning.

Everything had to be very 'pusser', as we called it: just how the Navy did it. You served the wet things, like the soup and the tea, on the right-hand side, but all the vegetables and the meat you served on the left-hand side. You stood to attention all the time in the wardroom if you weren't serving anybody. At lunchtime, the men would come in when they were ready, so you'd have three in at a time, maybe, and then maybe you'd get five or six all sitting down at once. It was just like a café, really. They got a proper hot meal, and then another hot meal at night. We served breakfast. That would be bacon and eggs and cereal of some sort — porridge, possibly. If they knew they were coming up for lunch they had to sign in the day before, but if they didn't know then they just turned up. Some were regulars, they lived in.

Was the Navy hierarchical?
Very, oh very. You couldn't go out with an officer, but some of the girls did, mind you. They were mostly girls who had the 'hook', as we called it, a petty officer.

Was it hierarchical within the Wrens as well?
Yes. The petty officers stuck together. Mary Morton was our Chief Petty Officer in the officers' quarters,

and she ruled us all with a rod of iron, but she was really quite nice when I got her away from the Navy. We became quite friendly.

There were married women. Our petty officer, Mary Lee, her husband was in the desert and he was killed, so she was a widow when she was in the Navy. Most of us were very young. Miss Duthie was the superintendent of Wrens on *Philomel*. She had grey in her hair. She was a very strict, attractive lady. Her right-hand man was Lorelle Corbin. She had more to do with us, and she was very strict. We were a bit scared of Lorelle. You saluted them when you met them anywhere. Even in the street you had to salute them if you were in your uniform. We liked doing that. You had to salute in the correct manner. If you didn't, you would be hauled up.

Did you have to wear identification tags?
Yes, they were very unprepossessing. They were, well, it wasn't plastic in those days, but it was some sort of material, red, with our name and rank and number on it. We wore those round our necks on a chain.

We had to have short hair. I always had a great problem because I had such a lot of hair and it wouldn't stay under my cap. I think the first winter we had the slouch hat and then they brought in the sailor's caps, like the sailors wore. In the summer we had white covers and we'd put them over the black hat, so they were very hot, but they were smart and didn't blow off. We had chin stays, which were the piece of ribbon tucked in underneath the crown, and when the wind blew, which it often did at Devonport, we'd pull our stays down and keep the hats on. They rolled beautifully, being that shape. Our clothes were beautiful, and it meant you weren't spending much on your clothes all through the war. I saved up a lot of money and had quite a nice little nest egg. I remember I bought my first Elna sewing machine when I left the Navy with some of the money.

Once a month, or was it once a week, we'd have to go on a route march. That started down in the naval base and we marched along Devonport to the shops and up the hill and then along past the Wrens' quarters. Then we'd go right round to another road that goes to Takapuna. We'd walk for miles in our heavy skirts and our thick grey lisle stockings and our big heavy shoes, and our hats and our gloves. The whole lot.

We also had to get ready for marches down Queen Street. We did that a couple of times too, on special days. It was a long march down Queen Street, but we loved that, it was fun.

As well as serving in the wardroom, Heather was also responsible for looking after one of the medical officers at Devonport.

When would you clean his room?

In the mornings, after breakfast, I'd go and make the bed, and change the linen. We blacked officers' shoes before we gave them their morning cup of tea. We took a morning cup of tea up to them, and a biscuit. I'd black his shoes while he was still asleep, you see, and then tap on the door and take him his tea. While he was in the bathroom, I'd lay out all the things that he was going to wear that day on his bunk. We really looked after them. I was his batman, really, if he were in the Army.

You were basically his servant.

Yes! And I didn't fancy that. I'd been brought up in Malaya with servants of my own!

I waited on him at table and looked after his clothes and so forth. When they were at work, once we were off duty from the wardroom, we changed into our navy blue overalls and my jobs were looking after his cabin, and cleaning the billiard table. There was a little ante-room where the officers brought their lady friends for a meal, and I had to tidy that up and see it was all in order. I also had to vacuum

Wrens practise signalling. Note their sailor caps.
ATL, PAColl-8844

all the lower level of the entrance hall and up the stairs, and clean the men's toilet, which was just sort of poked in behind the staircase.

It was a real eye-opener for me because I had absolutely no idea that men had quite a different set-up in the toilet department from women. I went into this room for the first time and thought, Whatever are those funny things hanging up on the wall? And there's a great big trough underneath it. What do they do there? Wash their feet? I wasn't going to ask anyone what all this strangeness was. I had some stuff to clean it with, so I sloshed a bit down the trough, and wiped those funny looking things hanging up, did the handbasins and then departed.

The trouble was that some of the officers really drank a lot. They would have a wonderful party

The ferry Kestrel *approaches Devonport wharf.* Special Collections, Auckland City Libraries, 1-W40

amongst themselves or with the girlfriends, and play billiards and get very, very drunk. They were all young too, and didn't know when to stop. So not only did the billiard table suffer, but the latrines were something else. It was more than I could bear. It was just so awful. Anyway, I did it. I must have done it for some months before my mother said, 'What's the matter? You always seem so upset when you come home.' I said, 'I've been cleaning the latrines at the naval base and it's so disgusting. Such and such an officer was sick all over the billiard table and was sick all over the latrines.' My mother didn't tell me, but she must have rung up Miss Duthie to say that she didn't think it was on that her daughter — her daughter! — was cleaning the men's toilets. The next thing I knew I was taken off toilet duty and a young matelot from the naval base came up and did them instead.

I had to not only clean the billiard table, I had to iron it. That was a lovely job. I enjoyed that and made it last. There was a little radio in there and I'd have Aunt Daisy on every morning. It was great fun. I'd do that table to within an inch of its life until I had to go and find something else to do. It was a dear little iron — a piece of flat iron with a handle, and you warmed it up on a little electric warmer. It was very thin. I suppose it wasn't more than about 10 centimetres in width. You put it on the warming plate and then you ironed the table. It would get cold very quickly, so it took quite a long time to get it heated, do the ironing and then put it back to get enough steam up to do a bit more of it. It all had to be one way. It was a full-size billiard table in a special billiard room, built for the officers. They did very well through the war, really. They lived like kings in that place.

We were on the run from dawn till dusk, we didn't need exercise. And in between whiles we were walking all the way from the naval base to the ferries, and then up and down Queen Street catching trams, going for miles. We did so much walking. There were very few cars on the road. For one thing there wasn't any petrol, and the other was that not so many people owned cars. We had to walk or go in trams, and trams only went in certain places, so wherever you lived, or wherever your friends lived, it could be another 20, 30 minutes walk away from the nearest tram stop. So we walked an enormous amount, and that kept us fit.

You were involved with the Wrens' Show, weren't you?
I don't know how that happened. We must have got together and had a bit of a discussion about what we might do. I can't remember, but I imagine it was up on our noticeboard, and we signed in if we thought we would like to be part of it. The buzz went round and we got a lot of people wanting to do

Hawaiian number in the Wrens' show. Heather is middle left, looking out of the frame.
Peter and Heather Crispe collection

things. I think the officers got it going. It must have been Miss Duthie, maybe Lorelle Corbin. They were the only two women with officer rank. The rest of the girls were petty officers, that's a non-commissioned rank. I don't really know how it all evolved. Certainly it was a load of fun and we really did enjoy doing that.

Was it a sort of variety show?
Yes, it was. Elaine Chambers sang solos, probably something like 'Berkeley Square' and 'The White Cliffs of Dover', some of the Gracie Fields songs. We did a Hawaiian number and that was 'Lovely Hula Hands', 'Blue Hawaii' and 'Hawaiian Moon', I think it was. I played the ukulele. My wonderful ukulele that was so useful for such a long time in the Navy. My dentist had been to Hawaii and bought the ukulele and didn't know how to play it, and he gave it to me for some unknown reason. It stood me in such good stead, because I was always in demand for the music when we were going on a trip with the boys and girls to a dance somewhere in the back of a lorry. We'd all sing. We were always singing.

It didn't matter who we were — whether we were Army, Navy, Air Force or just civilians — we all sang a lot during the war. All the old tunes. I knew them on my ukulele and kept everybody in tune. Everywhere I went, so did my ukulele.

In my particular show, I was the showman. It was really only me talking for about 10 minutes. I had waxworks, something like Madame Tussaud's. There were the three witches from *Macbeth*, and King Arthur and his knights. Bluebeard featured largely, and all his wives were hanging up with their heads chopped off on a white sheet and blood coursing down the sheet. It was great fun and everybody loved it. The sailors roared with laughter. It was such a good little show that we played it there for several nights in the naval base, and then we went to Motuihe Island. And I think we did it somewhere else — it might have been up at Whenuapai for the airmen.

We went to a dance at Whenuapai the night before my father returned from the camp in Siam. I was so excited. The last time I'd seen him, seven years before, he'd given me a watch, and I'd kept that watch faithfully all through the war and loved it dearly. The tide was out when we got to Hobsonville and their jetty was very high up out of the water. Because the boat was so low down with no tide, the sailors pulled us up by our arms, and evidently my dear old watch fell in the water. It was such a strange thing that I should lose it the very night before my dad came back to us.

Tell me how you found out about your father coming home.

I had a couple of cousins who were in the Navy and slipped in and out of Devonport from time to time. One of them, Peter Jerram, was a surgeon commander and happened to be there at the time when the Japanese capitulated. He said, 'Heather, Heather', as I served him with his soup. 'I've just heard through the radio in the naval base that your dad's all right and he's up in Kanburi camp. He's all right. He's all right.' That was the first we'd heard. I went to the telephone and rang Mother up. 'Peter's just heard that Dad's OK. He's OK. He's up in a camp in Kanburi.' I suppose Mother nearly fainted at the thought.

Had you heard from him at all?

No, only scruffy cards, and I think the last one we'd had had been about two years previously. So we had absolutely no idea if he was still alive. The cards were useless, they didn't say anything. They weren't even in his writing.

How long was it after that that your father came back to New Zealand?

As soon as Peter Fraser, the Prime Minister, heard that there were men in that camp, and I suppose other camps as well, he sent a special Dakota up. They arrived very quickly after we heard that he was alive. I'm sure it wasn't any more than a week.

They must have gone to Singapore first, then Brisbane. He rang us up that night. First time we'd ever had an overseas call, because they were rare in those days. And Mother heard her beloved's voice. The feeling was unbelievable, really. I hadn't seen the dear man for seven years. It was really quite strange. I think I had to be a bit forced in my feelings toward this strange man because I didn't know him. I was excited because that's what we'd been fighting the war for — to get Pa back — but I think I was a bit overcome. My sister wasn't so bad, because she'd been up to Malaya and stayed with them in Malacca just before the war, so she'd seen him quite recently before the war started. It was only something like four years that she hadn't seen him.

That was a wonderful moment in our lives. I thought, Whatever else I've done, I've done my bit for the war and we've got Pa back.

He flew to Whenuapai?

Yes, and they brought him down on one of the boats and landed at Admiralty Steps. I've got a picture of him standing there, this tall, gaunt-looking man in his old hat. He had a new uniform, but he still had his old hat. He was such a wonderful man. Full of stories. He talked for six months about the war, and then that was it. He didn't talk about it any more. He went back to Malaya and started things going again in the Survey Department.

Despite being in the Navy, Heather was one of the majority of wrens who did not spend any time at sea.

I went out for a day into the Hauraki Gulf, on target practice for the anti-aircraft guns on board the USS *Redpoll*. That was a lovely day. It wasn't rough, and we watched the little aircraft flying past with what they called a drogue. It was a long rope with an aircraft sock tied on the back, and they were shooting at that. That was quite exciting. We were given a shell case as we left, which I still have. I think there were about eight of us went aboard the *Redpoll*.

Was that the only time that you were on manoeuvres?

That I ever went to sea, yes, apart from going across in the ferry and other little boats to various places in the harbour. We were definitely shore-based only. We were to take the place of a sea-going man, whether he be an officer or a matelot. That was the idea: to release them from any shore duties so there were more to go away. We took on all the things that the men would have been doing — including the latrines!

Heather recalls the celebrations at the end of the war.

First of all we had VE Day. I don't remember too much about that, but I know we were all celebrating and really joyous at the thought that that was over. But we were still in the throes of all the Jap stuff, so it didn't make such an impression. We were still going to be needed in the Navy. When VJ Day happened, well that was a different kettle of fish altogether. Everyone rushed into Queen Street. I must have been off-duty that day, and my sister Claire left the office and came home. We rigged up a party. We shipped Mother out to visit some friends elsewhere, and didn't let on we were going to have a party because she wouldn't have let us. Everybody brought lots of beer. We had a wonderful party. We were so happy, we didn't go to bed, any of us. There must have been about 20 of us at home. Everyone went home at about six o'clock in the morning. We'd had a lovely time.

It was another six months or so before Heather was discharged. In the meantime, she had transferred to the dental section at Devonport.

I didn't make a very good dental nurse. There was a lot of dental work to be done, because some of the men hadn't been near a dentist for years. They'd been at sea all the time. The dentist that I worked for was a young chap, and he was rough. Every time the sailors were being drilled, or had a tooth pulled, or anything, what happened to me? I fainted. I couldn't bear to think that they were hurting them so much.

I wasn't any use at those moments, so they thought, Right. We'll put paid to this silly Wren's rubbish. We'll take her up to the operating theatre where we're going to take out every single tooth in the next sailor's head. Under anaesthetic they weren't hurting, so I was absolutely fine.

I didn't turn a hair. I didn't mind the blood, it was just the fact that I could see them being hurt because there were no injections being given or anything.

Even though dental repair work was done when required, the dental section spent a lot of its time extracting the men's teeth and then providing them with dentures.

Having false teeth in those days was quite a common occurrence. The dentists didn't take care of your teeth like they do these days. It meant that there were lots of dentures around the place because the teeth they put in very quickly got too loose because the gums shrunk. Then you needed another set and probably another set, so all these spare sets were hanging round the place. They were put away in boxes and drawers.

We had a long walk from the dental surgery down to the Devonport wharf every day. This one day it was very cold and I had my big coat on and was carrying my big blue bag with a zip. We all had these bags in the Navy. Our ditty bags, we called them. I had my card for the ferry boat — we had special cards — either in my coat pocket or inside the bag. This day, I fished round in my pocket, and it wasn't in my pocket so I thought it must be in my bag. As I pulled my hand out of the pocket, out came a couple of sets of teeth which clattered down on the floor in front of the people also running to catch the ferry. I gathered up these things and put them back in my pocket, then unzipped the bag and scrabbled round looking for my card, and what flew everywhere? About a dozen set of chompers, all over the floor by the ticket man. All the people gathered behind me, waiting to get through, gazing at this silly Wren with teeth all round her. It was embarrassment no end, but I had to laugh because it was very funny. They and the ticket man helped me scoop them up. What a mean lot of girls, weren't they? How they could do that to me!

Dad had gone back to Malaya and we were thinking of going too. I had to wait for my discharge. I'd had the medical examination and went home full of joy thinking, Now we can get on with things. I've left the Navy, we'll go to Malaya, which was so exciting to even think about. There was a tap at the door, and there was a lady in uniform. She said, 'I'm your health officer.' I said, 'I beg your pardon?' 'I need to come in and talk to you about something in your medical results.' We brought her in and she said, 'I'm very sorry to tell you, but you've got a shadow on your lung.' It was TB, but they didn't say that out loud.

One of Heather's petty officers, Mary Lee, had left the Navy because of tuberculosis and died soon afterwards. As a result, around nine of the Wrens who had worked with her had problems when they left the Navy. Heather was not allowed to work for at least six months and had to have X-rays and blood tests each week at Greenlane Hospital.

It was a huge great dagger of a needle and a great big syringe, about six inches long, and that was filled up with all your precious blood.

Heather eventually went to Malaya and had been there for a couple of years when she contracted cerebral malaria. She was extremely ill with a very high temperature for two or three weeks, but the worst thing was that it started her tuberculosis again, so she had to return to New Zealand.

US First Lady Eleanor Roosevelt inspects Wrens at Devonport, 1943. ATL, John Pascoe Collection, F-2034-1/4

I had a wonderful time in Malaya. We danced all night. We had servants in the house and that was wonderful for me. What a contrast to the Navy! I went to England in 1953 for the coronation. Everyone was on top of the world. We were going to have a lovely new queen, and it was a new era of peace and happiness and prosperity, and everybody was happy. People were whistling in the street and everything was getting under way again. The world was returning to normal. There were ships to travel on and new ships being built, and aeroplanes were coming into their own because now we could use all the expertise from building the aeroplanes during the war. Everything was good. People had work. It was a riotous time. The young people were all having a ball. Lots of people coming over from New Zealand. Those were the beginnings of the big OE and girls were coming over in groups. It was lovely. Nothing bothered us. It was great. I think it was the same with many people. They were getting on with their lives, having lovely romances, and their boyfriends and husbands were not going away to war.

Heather married her husband Peter in 1954 and the couple returned to New Zealand in 1958. They have two sons and a daughter.

Index